# *Organizational Mental Floss;*

# How to Squeeze Your Organization's Thinking Juices

## Lindsay Collier

May, 2014

ISBN-13: 978-1496069153
ISBN-10: 1496069153

## Prologue

This book has been in my head for what seems like a very long time. It was about 80% complete when my wife of 40 years, Jan, was diagnosed with ovarian cancer. I then devoted all of my time to caring for her with the hope that we would do all we could to help her recover. We didn't win this battle and I lost Jan along with much of my motivation to continue this book. I wrote a book called *Jan's Rainbow* and later a Kindle version, *Surviving the Loss of Your Loved One*. This was great therapy for me in dealing with my loss and also helped to keep my writing spirit alive.

I'm happy to say that my motivation to complete this book finally returned. I've had a long, rewarding career as an expert in creativity and innovation in a major corporation followed by one of consulting and speaking. I feel honored to have the opportunity to share what I've learned with you in the hopes that it will help you discover new ways to enhance creativity and innovation in your work and your lives.

My best to you, Lindsay

Here are a few things people have said about Lindsay's previous books.

"I laughed, I cried, it became a part of me! Well, actually, I lied about the crying part. Throughout this book, I found Lindsay's wit enjoyable and to the point. He had me smiling and, sometimes, laughing out loud. I saw parts of corporate America on almost every page (but never my company!?!?!?). I'm already using some of the ideas, so it really did become a part of me!
Dave Gunby, EDS

I was asked to review a video and book of Lindsay's for an upcoming speaking event. As I read excerpts from the book, I started to share them with other marketing managers and, from there, the book had a life of its own. For three days I chased it as it made frequent appearances in many offices with the telltale phrase, "Did you read this? This, us, them, or we use to .....!"
Carl Morrison, Burndy Electrical, Manchester, NH

Focused on challenging the way we think both "about" and "inside" our organizations, Lindsay has a unique and successful way of sharing his extensive experience and knowledge about transforming organizations.
Dr. Robert Ruotolo, Allied Signal Aerospace,
Phoenix, AZ

The Whack-A-Mole Theory is one of the most enjoyable books I've read on creativity and innovation. Lindsay knows what he's talking about and presents it in a fun, readable, and practical manner. He presents a very honest and thorough look at problems in organizations and how one goes about solving them. I loved this book and consider it a valuable tool for implementing organizational change. This is a must read for anyone who is interested in increasing their general level of creativity and innovation.
Susan Linscott, General Mills, Minneapolis, MN

This book is fun! Lindsay's unique writing style, combined with his insights and ideas, capture the essence of creativity. It's a must read!
Jim Lang, Parkridge Hospital, Rochester, NY

3

# Why you should buy this book

Books about business and organizations are not known as being a lot fun to read. As a matter of fact, some are downright dull and painful. I know because I've read a lot of them. This book is different. Where most other business books deal with the *left brain of business* this one deals with the *right brain*. This is your chance to really "air out" that hemisphere of your brain that you've been checking at the gate each morning. Where most business books take old ideas and rearrange them, this book is chock full of new and exciting ones. Ideas that will be useful to managers, professionals, teams, facilitators, engineers, product developers, marketers, and virtually anyone who would like to see an exciting future for their organization. Where most business books focus on behavior and results this one concentrates on thinking. And thinking occurs before anything happens. If you think dull thoughts there's a good chance you'll get dull results. On the other hand, if you think creative and exciting thoughts you may begin to get things you never imagined. This book will help you do just that. As someone once said, if you always use the same recipe, you'll always get the same bread. This book will give you a new recipe for organizational change.

I hoped I've piqued your interest somewhat. If you're still not convinced then take a quick look at the table of contents that gives a nice short summary of the chapters. Then check out the Appendix which by itself is worth the price of this book. Notice up front where it says, "copy until your toner runs dry". I consider it a complement every time you copy something of mine (besides that I use to work for company that made copy machines) and so I've put things in the Appendix that I thought would be useful to you. Oh sure, I'd love it if you called me up and asked me to come share some of this great stuff in person. But the next best feeling is that of knowing that you're benefiting from the ideas in this book while I'm hugging my wife, out playing golf or working on my next book.

Have fun and let me know how well you liked it. If you'd like to explore some of the thoughts and ideas in this book and want me to help you and your associates build their creative thinking skills please get in touch with me. We'll talk. I'll buy the coffee.

Lindsay Collier
lindsaycollier@comcast.net
amazon.com/author/lindsaycollier
lindsaycollier.weebly.com

"Every great oak was once a nut that stood its ground"

# Table of Contents

## Organizational *Tensegrity* and the Journey of Discovery

Here we lay the groundwork for creating an organization that has the capability of doing things they never thought were possible. We'll take a very different look at the mismatch between the nature of organizations and the characteristics that encourage creativity and innovation and we'll look at a process that will help close that gap.

## Where New Thinking and Ideas Come From

If you've ever wondered about the real sources of ideas, here's where you'll find them. Some may be very surprising! You'll see dozens of real life examples and leave this chapter with some exciting new prospects about where to find those idea treasures and some great ideas on how to trigger new ideas before their time.

## A Left-Brain Look at the Right Brain: Creative Thinking Process Overview

This is the best summary you'll ever see of some of the most powerful techniques for thinking creatively. A rational organization of what expands into hundreds of techniques that could generate ideas worth millions – no, make that gazillions!

## Chapter 4

## Group Mental Gymnastics and Warm-ups

If you are looking for a refreshingly different way to warm people up to some great thinking you'll find it here. This is a veritable candy store for facilitators of creative group activities. Warming up before physical activity is recommended practice. So why shouldn't you warm up before mental activity? The techniques here will free up the creative juices and really get you started – or they might get you fired.

## Chapter 5

## New Off the Wall Techniques for Stimulating Ideas

And now for something completely different! This is for those of you who are ready to temporarily lose all touch with reality and really get outside that thinking box. Some of you will find returning to reality very disappointing after taking some of the trips included here. Over the years I've used hundreds of ways to help people stretch into the creative zone. Here's where I get a chance to share some of these with you. Facilitators will really eat this one up!

## Chapter 6

## Getting Off the Beaten Path.
## Miscellaneous Organizational Braindroppings.

Here's my chance to let my mind wander into the discussion of a number of items that have intrigued me over the years. You'll find a wide array of ideas here that go from valuable observations on organizational life to the down right weird. Read a few of these *braindroppings* just before going to sleep each night and you'll feel great in the morning. Read a few more each morning and you'll feel great all day. What more could you want? These are great to use as abstracts in newsletters too. Just tell people where you got them.

## Chapter 7

## Scouting the Future

Back to earth! Pulling yourself to an exciting future is much more interesting than pushing yourself forward from today. Most organizations I've known tend to walk backwards into the future. Most of their energy is focused on protecting the past. Try to picture a cowboy backing away from the *bad guy* with guns blazing and you'll get a good picture of what I mean. Here we'll take a look at how to scout the future and its implications to you and your beloved organization. I'll also put my content futurist hat on and give you some great tips about the future.

## Chapter 8

## How to Be a Raging, Inexorable, Thunder-Lizard Idea Generator

You'll get to this chapter with hundreds of exciting ideas and possibilities. Here we'll look at how to really put them to use. You wouldn't want these great ideas to end up in *idea heaven* would you? Here we focus more on your own personal potential to be as creative as possible. After reading this chapter you'll actually be able to leap tall buildings in a single bound!

# Appendices

*There's a gold mine of information and ideas here. Copy them till your toner runs dry.*

## Appendix A

## Future Trends

For those who are interested in pursuing a more intensive process of scouting the future here is a rather complete summary of what futurists are saying. If you want a quick peak at future trends, driving forces, and technologies that will be important to you then cheat a little and turn to this appendix now.

## Appendix B

## A Few of My Favorite Quotations

Quotations are valuable thinking aids and here you'll find some of the best and most useable of all. In case I haven't told you yet, I have another book devoted to creative quotations (Quotations to Tickle Your Brain). Check it out. There are lots of laughs and lots of pearls of wisdom here that will help you take your thinking to a higher plane.

## Appendix C

## Museum of Bonehead Remarks

Talk about thinking blocks! Here's my collection of comments that illustrate how people have framed their possibilities based on their past experience (and usually been stung by it). Many of these will surprise you. Of course, none of you would ever think of saying anything as silly as what exists here in this Appendix. Doesn't it comfort you to know that the term 'bonehead' always refers to other people? I dare you to start reading this right now. Betcha can't stop!

## Appendix D

## How to Be Incredibly Creative All the Time

What more can I say? Keep these with you all the time. Hang them on your refrigerator. Put them under your pillow. Stick them under your eyelids. You'll never have the same *thinks* again.

## Appendix E

## Design of Creativity and Humor Rooms

I had my 15 minutes of fame when I built a Humor Room at Eastman Kodak in 1991 that was the precursor of many of the creativity rooms you see in organizations today. NBC Today, the Wall Street Journal, CNBC's Industry Week Managing Today program and write-ups in a number of magazines followed and a lot of companies began creating similar spaces based on this model.. Here are some thoughts for designing such a room for some really *funtastic* results.

## Appendix F

## Biography of Readings on Creativity

This may be the best book you ever read on creativity in business. But there are some other wonderful ones and I want you to read them all (after you read mine of course). I also don't want you wasting your time and money so there are some brutally honest reviews included.

## Appendix G

## New Job Titles

One way to be more creative is to change your title to something that really gets you excited. This is the best (maybe the only) collection of wild job titles you'll ever see. If you can't find that new title here then you can't find it anywhere. Feel free to use any of these titles for your own business cards.

## Appendix  H

## Things to Whine About

If you ever need a list of things to whine about, here it is. Whining about everything on this list is just like receiving an exorcism. And I'm beginning to think that we need more workplace exorcisms.

## Appendix I

## Murphy's Laws of Combat Operations

I'm not sure where I got these from but so many of them have a direct implication for all organizations. Most of them are also pretty funny.

## Appendix J

## Interesting facts

These are a blast! Some are quite amazing, some are very useful metaphors, and some are marginally useless but fun to know anyway. I've been collecting them for a long time and it feels good to be able to share them with you.

# Introduction

## "Oh the Thinks You Can Think"

It may sound very strange to start a book about real organizations with a quote from Dr. Seuss. Early in my career as an internal consultant at Eastman Kodak Company when I was in the first stages of developing of a program to train people in creative thinking my kids were at the "read me a story Daddy" stage (I wish I could go back there today). Of course, Dr. Seuss played a prominent role here and his book, *Oh the Thinks You Can Think*, gave me tremendous motivation to move forward and influence the thinking processes within this one-time great company.

Very few organizations I know of spend much time enhancing the thinking capabilities of their associates. Everything we do, individually and collectively, starts as a thought, becomes a behavior, and then moves to an action. I believe most organizations focus their energy on the behavior and the action. And yet, if they could jack up the thinking to higher creative level, tremendous possibilities would appear. Dull thinking creates dull behavior, which creates dull results. This book will help you to influence the thinking part of this flow and allow some much more creative behavior and results.

Why have so many of the programs of the past been so ineffective? Lately more and more is publicized about the failure of everything from TQM to reengineering or building learning organizations. Most of these failures come from the fact that, while many of these programs had the potential to be quite valuable, the real thinking within the organizations didn't change. Only behaviors and results were taken into consideration. When the thinking doesn't change, as soon as the program push stops, the path of least resistance takes you back to where you were. Unfortunately, it often takes you back to a position worse than you were before because you've most likely eroded the feelings, confidence, and morale of associates along the way. You've created disgruntled employees out of *gruntled* ones. I know of one major upstate New York company that has been nearly destroyed by the reengineering done by a major consulting firm. Major consulting firms tend to be pretty heartless and seem to have no concept of the dynamics that a *hatchet* job has on an organization.

Most of these programs are directed towards what CK Prahalad and Gary Hamel in their book, *Competing for the Future*, would call *managing the denominator*. If an organization's profit and viability are determined by the goods or services sold over the cost of these items, most organizations spend more time looking at the cost. Why not spend the time looking at how to increase the numerator (goods and services sold)? This book is about doing just that. By tapping the creative potential of people in the workplace you release an enormous potential that may be largely unused. To do that you must do something very different - but, before that, you must also be able to *think* very different.

The following story says a great deal about how organizational dynamics shapes the thinking process. Does it sound familiar to you?

> In a cage there are five apes. In the cage hangs a banana on a string over some stairs. Before long, one ape will go to the stairs and start to climb towards the banana, but as soon as he touches the stairs, all the apes are sprayed with cold water,

14

After a while, another ape makes an attempt with the same result and all the apes are sprayed with water.

After a while, if an ape tries to climb the stairs, the other apes will act to prevent it.

Now, remove one ape from the cage and replace it with a new one. The new ape sees the banana and wants to climb the stairs. To his horror, all the other apes attack him. After another attempt and another attack, he knows that if he tries to climb the stairs, he will be assaulted.

Next, remove another of the original five apes and replace it with a new one. The newcomer goes to the stairs and is attacked. The previous newcomer takes part in the punishment with enthusiasm.

Replace another ape with a new one. The new one makes it to the stairs and is attacked as well. Two of the four apes that beat him have no idea why they were not permitted to climb the stairs, or why they are participating in the beating of the newest ape.

After replacing the fourth and fifth original apes, all the apes that have been sprayed with cold water have been replaced. Nevertheless, no ape ever again approaches the stairs. Why not?

"Because that's the way it's always been around here."

So cast aside your thoughts as to the way things are supposed to be. And cast aside the strong need you may have to make judgments of the material in this book. Replace your *why?*

*thinking* with *why not? thinking.* There are techniques and thought processes here that will take you places you've never been before. You may be tempted to just scan over some of them and say, "That's interesting". I invite you to take this material much further and try these techniques out in your own situation, particularly where group process is possible. At the very least, you'll have a wonderful time thinking this way - and there's a pretty good possibility that you'll enable some very powerful breakthroughs.

Some of you may be thinking, "We don't have time for this." I'm hoping that, by the time you finish this book, you'll be saying, "We don't have time not to do this,"

One of my first mentors (although he never knew it) was George Prince. He is the one that originally spawned my interest in business creativity over 40+ years ago. He once described creativity as an arbitrary harmony, an expected astonishment, a habitual revelation, a familiar surprise, a generous selfishness, an unexpected certainty, a formidable stubbornness, a vital triviality, a disciplined freedom, an intoxicated steadiness, a repeated initiation, a difficult delight, a predictable gamble, an ephemeral solidity, a unifying difference, a demanding satisfier, a miraculous expectation and an accustomed amazement.

Try to recognize these as you read on. Have fun, enjoy the journey, and prosper!

# Chapter 1

## Organizational Tensegrity
## And the Journey of Discovery:

Building a Climate of Curiosity in
Your Organization

# Organizational Tensegrity;
# A Key to Creativity and Innovation

I wish I had invented the word, tensegrity, but I'm glad to say that one of my heroes did. Buckminster "Bucky" Fuller frequently invented words to explain paradoxes involved in creativity and innovation and this was the word that helped him create the geodesic dome and other great inventions. It's a cross between *tension* and *integrity* and a suggestion that much strength can come if we can find the right balance between the tension that feeds creativity and the integrity that allows us to be collectively innovative. Think of all the possibilities that this word suggests relative to what takes place in organizations and how these impact creativity and innovation. There are numerous paradoxical behaviors within organizations, each of which challenges us to find the right balance to create a breakthrough environment. Where does your organization fit regarding these?

Tension -----> Integrity

Focus ------> Chaos

Serious -----> Weird and Humorous

Tight -----> Loose

Bolstering today's strengths -----> Creating tomorrow's possibilities

Empowering individuals -----> Strengthening teams

Letting ideas flow (creativity) -----> Innovating products from ideas

Focus on short term ---- > Focus on long term

Obsession with cost ---- > Obsession with products & services

We tend to think that it's best to be at either the left or right when, in fact, the most powerful position may be achieving a good balance between the extremes.

One of the blockages to tapping the creativity of people at work is the mismatch between accepted behavior and behavior that elicits real creativity. What were you doing the last time you had a great idea? Most people would say something like driving my car, sleeping, brushing my teeth, or taking a shower. It would be rare for someone to say he was in a meeting or she was sitting at her desk waiting for the big idea to come. The fact is that creative ideas generally come when you let go, daydream, fantasize, wonder, wander, laugh, get outrageous, and do other things which are discouraged in a normal workplace. Innovative new ideas often come from people who are outside the knowledge base surrounding the problems and opportunities being considered. One of my favorite Sydney Harris cartoons depicts a person walking into a brainstorming session saying, "What are we working on? I'm from Breakthrough Temporaries." NIH (not invented here) and the "been there, done that" syndromes are alive and well in most organizations and this blocks them from seeing many things outside their immediate thinking patterns. Why did musicians invent Kodachrome? Why was the automatic telephone dialing system invented by an undertaker? Why did a hand grenade manufacturer invent a common air bag device? Maybe it's because these people didn't know the rules yet, and that helped them see things differently from those in the business. Are there some situations in your business that could benefit from people who don't know the rules and are free to challenge them? Of course there are.

Another major blockage to creativity and innovation in organizations results from behaviors which are typical in many organizations. I've spent over 40 years helping organizations of

19

all types tap the enormous creative potential available to them. And I've made it a point to make careful observations of the personal and group dynamics that impact this potential. Here are a few of these observations.

## Reactive vs. creative orientation

One of my favorite memories as a teenager was playing the Whack-A-Mole game at the annual carnival in my hometown. The object of this game is to use a rubber mallet to whack wooden mole heads that pop up quickly and randomly through holes in the game table. This game presents an interesting analogy to the behavior of many organizations: looking at each day as a series of problems to be solved (moles to be whacked). When the game of Whack-A-Mole is over you are back where you started. You have a clear table, a little less money, and a feeling that you've accomplished something when, of course, you haven't. People at work who spend their whole day reacting to problems usually end up right where they started. They have created nothing and they have a great feeling of accomplishment without ever accomplishing anything. Creativity and innovation are only valuable when they support the creation of something and it is absolutely necessary to have a creative, rather than a reactive, orientation to put that creative potential to work. Observe your own work system. Is it reacting or creating? How might you produce a creative orientation in your own situation?

## Projecting the past rather than creating the future

This behavior can be particularly deadly in companies that have achieved great success in the past. It has been said, *"On the road to the future, there are drivers, passengers, and road kill."* Many successful companies are positioning themselves to be road kill or, at the very least, passengers, because all their energy is invested in protecting their past successes. The more successful a company is, the more they have to protect. This leaves little energy to scout the future and create breakthrough thinking to pull it forward to new possibilities. Small companies find it easy to gain *attacker's advantage* against larger companies that are in a *circle the wagons and protect* mode. Witness the birth of *YaHoo* search engines on the Internet. Why was this created by a couple of *creative hackers* rather than by a major communication firm?

## Playing with "what you can see"

Organizations are like icebergs. There's a tip above the surface that you can see and move around. But there's also a huge portion below the water that wants to maintain the status quo. We try to move the part that we can see in the direction of higher creativity and innovation but that which we don't see tends to hold us back. A participant in one of my South African workshops suggested another analogy, that of a hippopotamus in water. We see a little bit of the head and ears above the water but guess what happens when you try to push a hippo by his ears. If we try to move an organization toward higher creativity and innovation by paying attention to only what we see, that which we don't see will bring certain failure.

The word *organization* itself is likely to limit us from a particularly exciting conversation about the future. You need to change the way people think and, to do that, you must change the words they use. I often ask people in my workshops to discuss their organizations using composts piles, plates of spaghetti and meatballs, schools of fish, hard drives or a number of other interesting analogies. This helps them to challenge their existing assumptions.

# Working from the "comfort zone".

Most organizations are full of people whose primary interest is that of being secure and safe in their jobs. This need for security is reinforced by today's ever-present perceived dangers of reengineering, reorganizing and downsizing. But no breakthrough ever originates within the comfort zone, period! I've seen a frightening number of organizations that have had their innovative and creative capacity brought back to zero through reengineering programs. Companies that want to become creative and innovative must realize that they must have environments that allow for risk taking and mistake making. This is a total thinking shift for many organizations. WD 40 derived its name from the 40th attempt at developing a water-displacing lubricant. Does your environment allow for 40 learning experiences?

With these thoughts in mind, let's take a look at two organizations: one typical, the other innovative. Where does your organization fit and how might it move towards the innovative side?

In a typical organization:

> Risk is avoided
> Failure is considered bad
> It is always deadly serious
> *Sameness* is rewarded
> We always know the answer
> NIH (not invented here) is alive and well
> There is a judgmental attitude

In an innovative organization:

Risk is taken
Failure is a learning experience
Serious and fun are working partners
Leans toward diversity
Does a lot of wondering (what if?)
There is openess to thinking from outside
There is non-judgmental attitude

What would your organization be like if you could truly say it strongly fit all the characteristics listed in the second grouping? Many organizations like to say they are open, non-judgmental, and value diversity but, when the rubber hits the road, few really do. Many organizations claim they value fun in the workplace but few are really able to capitalize on the tremendous benefits of using positive humor that is firmly connected to the work. What can you do to make these characteristics come alive in your organization?

## The breakthrough model

Most organizations have a good idea of their current potential and this tends to limit their thinking. To move from current performance to the edge of your current potential is to become more perfect at what you know how to do right now. I call this *perfective change* and believe that's what the majority of organizations are working on right now. Certainly, becoming perfect at what you now do is a worthwhile endeavor. But the real opportunity for a great future often lies outside the area you normally think of as being possible. Moving into the breakthrough area beyond your perceived current potential is what I refer to as *transformative change*. It takes you to somewhere you haven't been before and unleashes possibilities you didn't even know you had. Just recognizing that a zone like that exists is the first step toward being able to get there. But, unfortunately, there are many things that keep most organizations from seeing and realizing this potential. How do organizations create opportunities in the breakthrough zone? Several things must fall into place in sequence. I refer to this as a *Journey of Discovery*.

- Create a compelling vision of the future.
- Question current thinking patterns.
- Create an environment for creativity and innovation.
- Build creative thinking skills.
- Scout the future.
- Let it happen.

## Create a compelling vision of the future.

Volumes have been written about visions and hours have been spent in meetings polishing vision statements. What I am talking about *is a simple statement that compels people to move forward.* I call this *Viper* or *Prowler* vision. I believe that Chrysler Corporation, whether they meant to or not, created a strong positive vision with their Dodge Viper and Plymouth Prowler. These cars have no particular reason for being as far as the economics of the business. But they do provide a powerful vision to these car divisions of what they are capable of doing. They are statements of vision. Let's face it - the name Plymouth didn't tend to give goose bumps to a car enthusiast. But seeing a *Prowler* did. It also turned on those involved in building the whole line of cars. In the end I guess it didn't help much since Plymouths are now a thing of the past but the impact on motivating Chrysler employees I believe was quite dramatic.

A while back I had the pleasure of spending a morning in a progressive township in South Africa, discussing some programs with the town's leaders. I asked them what their vision of the future was. Their response really floored me. They said, "We want to create a paradise in our township." This is a vision that drives people into the breakthrough zone. It's simple, visual, and powerful.

Visions can create futures that no one thinks are possible! Monuments are usually built to commemorate events or figures of the heroic past. But Geoffrey Stiflen, a young South African architectural student working on a graduate-studies project in the United States, decided to build one to the future. To a vision of a future South Africa which is being formed as black and white people come together in scores of different situations and work together to forge a new social culture.

Frank O'Conner, the Irish writer, tells in one of his books how, as a boy, he and his friends would make their way across the countryside. When they came to an orchard wall that seemed too high, too doubtful to try, and too difficult to permit their voyage to continue, they took off their hats and tossed them over the wall. Then they had no choice but to follow. A compelling vision can be as easy as envisioning those hats on the other side of the wall.

Sometimes visions are formed by making declarations about what you are going to achieve even before you're really sure you can achieve them. Edison boasted to the newspapers that he had just solved the problem of the subdivision of the electric light before he even had an operating bulb to exhibit. In 1991 I developed the concept of the Kodak Humor Room and plans for its development. I knew what I wanted to do but didn't really have approval to do it. The opportunity came up to interview the *Wall Street Journal* about his project and I went ahead and told them that we were going to build it. I had created the vision and now had no choice but to move forward to make that vision come true. A vision that comes from the fact that you've declared something is done is a powerful one. We would sometimes hold parties at the beginning of difficult projects, complete with victory celebration cakes, to give people the taste of success up front.

## Question the current thinking patterns

Albert Einstein once said, "The world that we have made as a result of the level of thinking we have done thus far creates problems that we cannot solve at the same level at which we created them." The major blockages to seeing future opportunities in the breakthrough zone are the many patterns, rules, and assumptions that filter what we are able to see. If we can somehow open our thinking and clear out these filters we can begin to see opportunities that were previously out of our view. The more established you are in your business, the stronger these blockages are and the more vulnerable you are to having breakthrough in your field come from outsiders who haven't yet *learned the rules.*

Organizations that attempt to shift these patterns, or paradigms, usually come up short of making real shifts. Rather than shift to new patterns they tend to merely enhance the existing ones. Just as racehorses wear blinders so they see only what's in front of them, organizations are built to travel the road they can clearly see and their track is often circular and this always takes them back to the starting point. Innovation can take place on the beaten path but the real, exciting opportunities can only be found off the beaten path. Are you traveling the beaten path in your organization and, if so, in what ways might you get off and explore the fascinating area beyond? Suggestions for exploring opportunities off the beaten path often come from outsiders and we quickly label these people as fools. When track coach Bill Bowerman suggested a waffle pattern to a sneaker manufacturer he was quickly told to stick to being a coach. He didn't, and Nike was formed. When a hand grenade manufacturer suggested a simple, inexpensive explosive device for triggering air bags, most auto companies told him to take a hike. He didn't – and he became a multi-millionaire.

In the late '80s Eastman Kodak was feeling threatened by impending advances in digital imaging. Huge success over many years had created a strong pattern of thinking that held that the only acceptable form of imaging was *chemical* imaging. Most efforts within the company in digital imaging were destined to be unsuccessful because managers simply didn't believe anything could be better than what had made them so successful in the past. Being stuck in a thinking pattern changes the old adage, "I'll believe that when I see it," to, "I'll see that when I believe it." Kodak didn't believe in digital imaging (even though they were instrumental in its development) and spent too much time trying to protect its existing business by "proving" that digital would never overtake chemical imaging. I was fortunate to be a part of a task force whose objective was to establish Kodak as a world leader in imaging and the major turnaround came when we were able to establish a thinking pattern that allowed them to see that digital was an opportunity, not a threat. This should have become the basis for a strong, compelling vision and a major thinking shift that would allow them to move forward toward a great future in both chemical and digital imaging. Unfortunately management decided to reject the thinking of our task force – and the rest is a very sad history of the fall of a once great company.

As a side note, it is interesting to note that the word "imaging" was never, or rarely, heard in industry a dozen years ago. Now this word encompasses the photographic business, the printing business, and information technology. This has created a real paradigm shift in the rules we share regarding this community of knowledge. New companies are able to get into the business because the old ones *go back to zero*. Whole new skill sets are required (digital vs. traditional photo skills). And change and innovation become the new drivers rather than becoming perfect at what you do. This suggests that one of the main issues in business is how to balance your time between planning current activities and planning continuance in your industry.

Thinking shifts don't have to be complex. As a matter of fact, they are often incredibly simple. How many engines does a car have? My thinking pattern tells me the answer is one. It's always been that way so most car designers assume that's the way it must be. Early developers of hybrids asked themselves why a car should have just one engine and the hybrids were born. They broke the rule and created a whole new set of opportunities! Are there any simple assumptions like this in your work that, if shifted, would have a major impact?

Where is your organization regarding its patterns of thinking? Are there certain assumptions about your business that are keeping you on the beaten path? What are some of the key problems that cannot be solved using the existing paradigms? What is impossible to do today which, if it were possible, would have a tremendous impact on your business? These are tough questions that deserve some probing. I've worked with dozens of organizations over the years helping them search for answers to these and other paradigm questions and am firmly convinced that this exercise is critical to creating a great future.

## Create a climate of curiosity

28

When we go back to the iceberg and the hippopotamus analogies it's important to realize that virtually all the organizational dynamics that affect creativity and innovation lie beneath the surface. Generating and bringing forward new ideas in organizations often brings out the worst behaviors in people. What was the reaction on the part of your associates last time you had a great, new, different idea? Chances are it was met with several *yah-buts* and other rather non-supportive comments. There is, unfortunately, a stronger tendency for people to be threatened by the creative ideas of their associates than to be genuinely supportive of them. In my 30 years' experience at all levels within organizations I've rarely seen people that provide all out support to other people's creative ideas. The floors of many organizations are covered with the remnants of bashed ideas. How might you create an environment that nurtures creativity in your own organization?

Start by evaluating where you are regarding the characteristics shown in Fig 1.3. Which of these need improvement and how might you go about making these improvements? Organizations must create an environment of inquiry that encourages genuine dialogue and allows for wondering, mind stretching, risk taking, positive humor, and a balance between individual-based and team-based creativity. The focus of many organizations is on teamwork and there are some terrific opportunities to enhance creativity in a team environment. But don't lose sight of the fact that individuals need personal recognition for their ideas and, if they think their ideas will just be absorbed as team ideas, may not contribute within the team environment.

Another critical creative environment issue is diversity within the thinking core of the organization. Ideas are often generated by groups of people who have virtually the same backgrounds and the same thinking characteristics. Marketing people generate marketing ideas, engineering ideas are generated by engineers, and so forth. In addition, we often select our most creative people to do this. There are two fallacies involved here. I've already discussed the need for diversity of knowledge. It is also important to create a good balance between people who are *dreamers* (right brainers) and those who are *realists* (left brainers). A group of dreamers can generate ideas *till the cows come home* and never accomplish anything. A group of realists can discuss the realities of bringing new ideas to life for the same amount of time and also never accomplish anything. There is also a need for *tensegritors* who are able to help bring new ideas to reality without losing the creative flair of these ideas. Do you have a good balance of these traits in your organization or team?

What are the real ingredients of organizational innovation? There are a number of academic studies of this but here's my list based on over 40 years of observation and experience helping organizations tap this great resource. Some of them might surprise you and there is some overlap between these items.

1. There must be **trust and support** within the organization. If there is no trust and respect for each other and people are unwilling to support the creative thinking of their associates, there is no chance for innovation! If people aren't open with each other, jealous of other's ideas, talk about others in negative ways, or just flat don't particularly even like their associates, you are pretty much guaranteed that all creativity and innovation will be stifled.

2. There is a **willingness to take risks and accept failure as learning experiences**. Fear of failure is one of the most powerful blocks to creativity. People will rarely stretch into

the creative zone if they think there is a good possibility of failure and that it will harm their future opportunities. The fear may come from a range of possibilities from real punishment (losing my job) to more subtle concerns (making a fool of myself). If people are pre-occupied with these worries there will be little creativity and innovation.

3.  The work must provide **significant challenge** and the ability to stretch thinking to places it's never been. A bridled mind is generally not a creative one. Few organizations really stretch the thinking capacity of their members. And many tend to burden their people with insignificant tasks requiring little creative input which results in much of their time being spent on *busy work*. Are people in your organization really challenged?

4.  There must be willingness to question accepted rules and assumptions. Areas of real breakthrough are often blocked by existing patterns of thinking. Remember the ***White Bread Warning***. If you use the same recipe, you'll get the same bread. Innovative organizations know how to question, and shift, existing assumptions, rules, patterns, and paradigms. And, they really enjoy the process of questioning and, perhaps, breaking the rules.

5.  There must be willingness to **value resources outside their field of knowledge**. The NIH (not invented here) syndrome must be cast aside. The illusion that the only good ideas are the ones that *we* have is very powerful in organizations. History shows that a large percentage of innovations come from outside the knowledge communities that you might expect (the ballpoint pen was invented by 2 Hungarian barbers, Kodachrome was the brainchild of 2 musicians, the

bikini was invented by a French engineer, etc.). There must always be a willingness to accept other's thinking.

6. There must be a **creative orientation** rather than a reactive responsive one. People in a creative organization have a positive spin on everything. They are playing to win and not playing "not to lose". They are creating their future and not protecting their past. If your organization has preponderance towards reactive problem solving there will be little time for creating anything new.

7. **Positive humor** must be valued as a resource. If people aren't getting real kicks out of what they're doing and having some laughs along the way, you might as well kiss the creativity goodbye. People need to be able to get loose and crazy and get into the *silly zone* often. The good news is that the ability to tap humor as a resource has many benefits apart from helping to tap creativity.

8. People must have a **passion** in their work. Where there is no passion there is no creativity. People just have a hard time conjuring up creative energy regarding things that don't turn them on. Passion is driven by an exciting, visual, attainable, stretch vision along with a good dose of self-confidence. Do these things exist for you and your associates? Do you have a way of helping people focus on their areas of passion?

9. **Creative idea stimulating techniques** must be understood along with the ability to use them in spontaneous ways. There are some wonderful ways to stimulate creative thinking for getting people into the *zone*. Skilled creative process consultants can bring out the best in the thinking capacity of you and your associates. And it's often best to bring one in

from the outside. That way you won't be facilitated by someone who may be compelled to live by the company rules.

10. There must be an understanding that creativity and innovation is not something you turn on and off with the flip of a switch. The **environment must exude creativity** in all aspects. It must look, sound, feel, and smell creative. Just entering the environment makes people come alive. In a creative environment, creativity and innovation are like garlic - no matter what you do, you can't shake it.

11. There needs to be a good balance of **dreamers, builders, and realists** and an appropriate balance of creative processes (expanding thinking) and innovative processes (making them real). If your entire group consists of all dreamers who love to ideate all the time but really don't like to bring anything to its innovative conclusion, nothing will be accomplished! If it's all realists who spend most of their time in relatively judgmental modes, there will also be little innovative output. Work to get a good mixture in the group.

12. The creative/innovative process must contain the ability to **scout the future**. Information about trends, drivers, technologies, and emerging capabilities in the future serves as some of the most powerful fodder for today's ideas. Pulling yourself toward some powerful future possibilities is much more exciting (and effective) than pushing forward from today's problems. My own experience is that few companies do a good job in this area, so the potential for an organization with these abilities is awesome.

13. There must be the ability to carry out processes with total **non-judgment**. Much easier said then done! Most of us seem to have a natural built in tendency to evaluate, even when it comes to our own thinking. It's difficult to listen to anything

without thinking about whether it's right or wrong. It takes a good amount of practice before we can truly take in information in a non-evaluative mode where there is no good or bad - only interesting. How might you bring out some non-judgmental behavior in your own situation?

14. **Fear of success** is also a blockage to creativity and innovation. People need to know that, if they create breakthrough through their creativity, they won't eliminate their job or compromise their future. This is particularly true of consultants - internal and external. I speak from experience on both ends. A consultant's job, in most cases, is to work themselves out of a job. This can be a hard pill to swallow so many consultants opt to recommend things that will lengthen the association with their clients.

15. The environment needs to provide opportunities for people to **play outside of their normal sandboxes**. There needs to be time to wander away from the normal work and wonder about just about anything. The law of connectivity suggests that nothing new is ever created. We just re-combine things in more creative ways so innovation involves finding those new combinations.

16. There must be a balance between **focusing on results and letting go**. Creative new ideas often come from getting away from the work while the desired goal sits around in the subconscious just waiting for some great connections. *If at first you don't succeed, give up* is often the best motto of creativity. Can your work environment accept this motto? What do you need to do to create opportunities for letting go?

17. There needs to be an appropriate balance between **individual and team feedback** and credit for creative thinking. If

34

individuals feel the credit for their own personal creativity will be given to a team, they will hold back. Creativity is often a fairly personal thing and a strong team environment may be very frustrating to some highly creative people who would like recognition for their ideas.

18. **Promises must be valued**. When we say we're going to do something, it must be done. This may sound a bit strange but, in most organizations, most promises can be written off right away. This practice must be changed if real innovation is to take place. In an environment where promises are meaningless there will be little chance for a lasting release of creativity and innovation. What is the quotient of kept promises in your organization?

19. There needs to be an **open flow of information** within the organization. Open book management gives people the full information and knowledge they need to build on using their creative/innovative capacities. It also opens up the desire of people to be open with their own creativity and ideas. Most people's capacity to give of themselves is strongly connected to their perception of how much information is shared with them.

20. The **physical environment** needs to be one that stimulates creativity. Surroundings need to be pleasant, interesting, humorous, and rich in visuals that entice creative thought. What can you do to add more excitement to your area?

Each situation requires a different amount of up front work regarding the analyzing and shifting of this environment. Following is a questionnaire which I frequently used in workshops to get people discussing where their particular needs are. Copy it and try it in your own team or organization.

# Group Climate of Curiosity

Rate your team or organization on a scale between zero and ten in each of the following categories. Zero means you are totally lacking in the category and 10 means you have an abundance of it.

### 1. Trust and support
0   1   2   3   4   5   6   7   8   9   10

### 2. Willingness to take risks
0   1   2   3   4   5   6   7   8   9   10

### 3. Work provides challenge
0   1   2   3   4   5   6   7   8   9   10

### 4. Willingness to question the rules
0   1   2   3   4   5   6   7   8   9   10

### 5. Valuing of outside resources
0   1   2   3   4   5   6   7   8   9   10

### 6. Creative vs. Reactive orientation
0   1   2   3   4   5   6   7   8   9   10

### 7. Valuing of positive humor
0   1   2   3   4   5   6   7   8   9   10

### 8. Passion in the work
0   1   2   3   4   5   6   7   8   9   10

**9.** Understanding of creative ideation techniques

0   1   2   3   4   5   6   7   8   9   10

**10.**
### Environment exudes creativity and innovation

0   1   2   3   4   5   6   7   8   9   10

**11.**
### Balance between dreamers, realists, and dreamers

0   1   2   3   4   5   6   7   8   9   10

**12.** Scouts the future

0   1   2   3   4   5   6   7   8   9   10

**13.**
### Ability to be non-judgmental

0   1   2   3   4   5   6   7   8   9   10

**14.**
### No fear of success

0   1   2   3   4   5   6   7   8   9   10

**15.**
### Provides opportunities to play outside the box

0   1   2   3   4   5   6   7   8   9   10

**16.**
### Balance between results and *letting go*

0   1   2   3   4   5   6   7   8   9   10

**17.**
### Balance between individual and team feedback

0   1   2   3   4   5   6   7   8   9   10

**18.**

**Promises are valued**

0

      1   2   3   4   5   6   7   8   9   10

**19.**

**Open flow of information**

0  1  2  3  4  5  6  7  8  9  10

**20.**

**Physical environment**

0  1  2  3  4  5  6  7  8  9  10

Use this questionnaire to start a dialogue about where you currently are in terms of a creative environment. If there are significant problem areas then you need to address them before going any further. It just makes no sense to try to build creative thinking skills in an environment that won't support them.

## Build creative thinking skills

Most of my experience comes from my years within Kodak where I trained hundreds of people to use creative thinking techniques. I believe we had one of the most unusual workshops in the country but, because the company was not prone to sharing this type of information, very few knew about them. Students need to know the basic characteristics of creativity and how organizational dynamics support or impede it. They need to understand how to create environments that will nurture creativity and they must also understand thinking patterns and how to shift them. Then the techniques of stimulating creative thought can be used to the maximum within their organizations.

Many consultants will tell you that all you have to do is teach people creative thinking techniques, send them back to the workplace, and let them go at it. Guess what? It won't happen! I've learned from experience that it takes a lot more than that so please don't make the same mistakes I did. Make sure the process for stimulating creativity and innovation in your organization goes well beyond just teaching creative thinking techniques. Make sure it also creates the environment for this thinking to survive.

Chapters 3-5 contain some very different techniques for stimulating group and individual creative thought that will help you take the thinking to levels never before achieved. Have fun with these but make sure you don't introduce them into an environment that isn't ready.

## Scout the future

The next step involves scouting the future, something very few organizations do. Those who think they do it rarely do it well. A recent *Fortune* magazine said, "In most organizations, the future doesn't have a lobbying group." Future scouting should always be a part of the creative and innovative backbone of an organization.

Wayne Gretzky once said, "I skate to where the puck is going to be, not to where it is." Most organizations I'm familiar with spend enormous energy following the puck around only to find out that, when they get there, it's gone. Doesn't it make sense to divert this energy to finding out where the puck is going to be?

Scouting the future starts with identifying potential events and trends in the future and assessing the current implications of these to your business. The final objective is using this information to develop a creative plan for the future. The events and trends of the future may shift at any time so it's worthwhile to stay in touch with the literature from futurists and their organizations. The World Future Society has a very good quarterly called *The Futurist* and they have a bookstore full of information about all aspects of the future. And Chapter 7 focuses on how to create future pull and has some of the most interesting stuff you'll ever read about this topic.

## Build a field and they will come

This statement comes from the movie, *Field of Dreams*. I want to leave you with this thought before we move on because it's very important. If you build a climate of curiosity you have the possibility of turning on creative, innovative powers that perhaps haven't been tapped in years. In other words, build a creative climate and the creativity will come. Let me know how you make out.

# Chapter 2

# Where New Thinking and Ideas Come From

Over the years I have spent a lot of time tracking the genesis of interesting ideas. When I see particularly interesting new ideas I try to track down the things that caused this idea to emerge. What happened just before this idea emerged? What things came together to cause the *eureka*? If we can define the things that really bring new ideas forth, we should be able to create techniques for bringing these ideas out before their time. For example, if ideas often come from things you trip over perhaps we can throw out a bunch of things to mentally trip over and force some new ideas to come out before we physically trip over them.

This chapter is about creating catalysts for new ideas. The most obvious use of these catalysts is in new product ideation but they will also give you lots of clues for generating ideas for any purpose. There will be some overlap between the different catalysts but that's okay. As you read them try to think about how you might design a way to force the process in a group setting. I'll include a few ways as well but doing this on your own would help you to build your own creative thinking skills.

## Catalysts for Emerging New Ideas

### 1. An innovative idea finds an application in another area.

The world is full of new and interesting innovations that have useful applications in other areas. Wander around a department or hardware store (or just wander through a catalogue) and jot down all the interesting things you see or just brainstorm them. Another great source for these triggers is Popular Science (particularly their *"What's New?"* section). Here are a few to get you started.

snake lights

salad spinners
CD ROM Telephone Books
ice scraper gloves
home ATM's
Swiss Army cards
disguised key holders
bright, crazy neckties
snore controls
sneaker pumps
peel and stick lenses
floating houses
window blinds

In each of these instances an interesting idea was transferred to some other area and applied. The question is how we can apply the general essence of a wide array of innovative ideas to a problem or possibility on which we are working. Can the snake light idea be applied to a camera? Of course it can - in a number of creative ways. How about the ice scraper glove concept applied to the camera? How might we apply the snake light idea to things other than products (such as motivating people at work, banking, creating a business plan etc.)?

How might we create an innovation that takes advantage of a relatively old idea like window blinds? A design group from New York City has developed the *Solar Blind.* This captures the solar energy it receives on flexible photovoltaic film and stores the energy in a rechargeable battery. At night, electro luminescent strips on the front edges of the slats glow to supply background ambient lighting to the room. Great idea, isn't it? What other possibilities can you think of here?

Anyone has the capability of preparing their minds for this kind of idea generation by keeping a data bank of these innovative

43

products and ideas and looking for connections. Later we'll look at some techniques designed specifically to make this happen in a group setting.

## 2.   A collision between a problem or opportunity and something that just happens to appear.

I was reading about a 10 year old girl that was decorating her Christmas tree and, while putting the angel on the top, heard a radio program discussing the high percentage of home fires that start from these trees. She happened to observe a smoke detector at that time and - bingo! She invented a Christmas tree angel with a built in smoke detector, called the *Guardian Angel*. Don't you wish you had thought of this? One of the interesting characteristics of new ideas is that they seem so obvious - after they're invented.

In another example of this, a man who was concerned about an extended garbage strike in New York City was wondering what he was going to do with his garbage. He was wrapping a birthday present and it occurred to him that a wrapped present on the streets of NYC has a very short life. You can probably guess the rest. He just wrapped his garbage as a present, put it on the sidewalk, and it's gone.

And the idea for flexible ice trays for the freezer came from an astute observer who noticed how easily ice fell from rubber boots when they were re-shaped. As someone once said, "Invention favors the prepared mind."

## 3.  Experiencing discomfort or tripping over something.

44

Warren Bennis said, "Every where you trip, a treasure lies" and Albert Einstein said, "In the middle of every difficulty lies opportunity." Where is there a better source for new ideas than in the problems we experience each day?

An 8-year-old boy from Victor, NY invented a product called the *Comfi-Rider*. While riding in the back seat of his family's van he often napped with his head against the window. To get more comfortable he would use a pillow that would usually slide down causing him to hit his head on the window. The simple idea of a pillow with suction cups to hold it on the windows seemed to work. A kindergarten girl who was tired of splashing herself by stepping in mud puddles at night invented a *Mudpuddle Spotter* - an umbrella with a flashlight attached to the handle that helps people see puddles in the dark. A first grader who was concerned about the safety of her classmates while walking along the road to the library invented the *Line Leader and Keeper*. It's a rope-like device with handles for children to hold onto. The teacher's front handle lights up and signals the teacher if a child lets go.

Charles King, on a trip to Florida realized his family was packing up four different half-empty suntan lotions, all sandy and gritty. He came up with the idea of *Tanning Kiosks* where sunbathers can be sprayed with a hose-like device with all the protection they need and avoid all the discomforts of greasy hands. He's spending a lot more time in the sun these days. Speaking of spending time in the sun, a 23 year old woman who was feeling rather depressed about her business decided to go and lay on the beach for a while. She put her sun tan lotion on and, as she laid down, a gust of wind picked up her towel and covered her with sand. Instead of relaxing she decided to try and solve this problem and invented a line of weighted beach towels. She sold 4.5 million dollars worth the first year and is not quite as depressed these days.

45

The wife of Johnson & Johnson cotton buyer, Earle Dickson, tended to be somewhat of a klutz and, whenever she cut herself, he would apply dressings and surgical tape. It was a two-handed operation so, when he wasn't home, he'd lay out strips of adhesive tape with gauze down the middle and would cover the exposed sticky surface to keep it from drying out. Whenever his wife cut herself she could simply cut off a piece of tape, remove the cloth and apply it. Thus, the *band-aide* was invented.

An undertaker in Kansas City invented the automatic telephone dialing system. At the time he was one of two undertakers in the city and it happened that the other one's wife was the telephone operator. When someone called looking for an undertaker guess which one got the job? In this case his survival depended upon getting the manual operators out of the process.

Howard Head was so frustrated with skiing that he decided to make some changes and ended up revolutionizing the materials and manufacturing in the ski industry. Another frustration with his off center tennis shots led him to inventing the oversized *Prince* racket.

Sometimes discomfort can be put to use. An isolated tribe in sub-Saharan Africa came up with a method for avoiding overly long speeches that they consider being injurious to both the speaker and the audience. The custom is that the speaker must stand on one leg while addressing the audience. As soon as his second foot touches the ground he must stop. Could you use this idea in any meetings of yours?

And, finally, Walter Lanz was on his honeymoon and constantly bothered by the loud pecking of a woodpecker outside their window. In the end it was a real blessing because this was the origination of *Woody Woodpecker*.

46

What are some of the things that you trip over each day? What are the discomforts you and your organization are experiencing (many of which you've probably learned to live with)? Keep a diary of these. Somewhere in each of these is the seed for an idea and, since you're probably not the only one experiencing that discomfort, it just may be one with widespread application.

**4.  A technology or idea that finds applications in a totally different area (cross fertilization).**

Recently there have been some breakthroughs cited in the detection of breast cancer using the technology from missile tracking. We don't normally bridge the gap between missile technology and health issues. Each problem or opportunity area typically works within its own sphere of knowledge. Why not try to break out more often? A key question might be "What are some areas of technology from areas well outside our problem"? We so often tend to think that the solutions to our problems and our new areas of opportunity are close by and rarely go looking in places that don't seem to be connected. What could people in the missile detecting business know about finding tumors? Probably not much, but they seem to be able to find targets and, after all, isn't a tumor a good target?

An article in *Compressed Air Magazine* called *Pressure Cooking Toxic Wastes* details a new technique called supercritical water oxidation. A derivation of the process of pressure cooking, it has promise of being a way to safely and totally destroy many of the hazardous materials that are by-products of our environment.

How might we apply snowmaking technologies to improve the world in which we live? A Canadian company has developed a

47

wastewater treatment called *Snowfluent* that gets rid of sewage by freezing it. From nozzles mounted on a tower, wastewater is sprayed at extremely high pressure. Tiny droplets instantly crystallize in the cold air and fall to the ground as snow forming piles up to 50 feet high. The rapid crystallization ruptures the cell membranes of bacteria and other microorganisms, destroying them and other contaminates which are naturally absorbed into the ground.

One of the most interesting cross-fertilizations of technology is the use of gasoline anti-knock compounds (methyl tertiary butyl ether) for breaking down gallstones. Fill me up with high test please. And researchers at Los Alamos are working on the development of refrigeration by loudspeakers. Now there's a unique thought. Hey Honey, let's spend tonight listening to the milk cool.

Sometimes we find rather unique uses of fancy technologies that actually bring them down a few pegs from their original inventors intended usage. The National Laboratory is currently developing new laser devices for removing graffiti based on laser technology. This is a technology that was originally developed to create weapons powerful enough to vaporize incoming missiles. Down to earth problems, like removal of graffiti, rarely warrant new technological inventions. Perhaps we should be spending more time asking how we might apply various high technologies to our low technology problems.

One of the unique characteristics of this source of new ideas is that it is derived from a totally new set of competencies. Companies that you'd expect to be developing new refrigeration systems have no advantage if the shift is to refrigeration by sound. As a matter of fact, they probably have a fairly healthy disadvantage because they are stuck in their old thinking patterns.

The developers of the digital watch had an easy road because the dominating Swiss watch industry could not even accept the fact that the future of watches could be anything else than the mechanical designs they had mastered through the years. In the end, all they could do is *watch* as their industry was literally taken over by complete newcomers to the business. That's why it's so important to create the awareness of this form of new idea generation. That's also why it's so important to enable companies to challenge their existing thinking often. When the paradigm shifts, everyone goes back to zero. It breaks my heart to say this since I had a fairly long history with the company, but Kodak is perhaps one of the best examples of this.

What are some technologies that may have applications in something you are working on? Start with technologies that would appear to be well outside the area of your interest because these may supply some of the most interesting possibilities. Here are a few technologies to start you off. Add to this and create your own list and don't make any attempt to stay within your own area. As a matter of fact, it's probably much more useful to be well outside your own area. Don't worry; you don't even need to know anything about the technologies. There are always people who love to be asked about their technologies and would jump at the chance of finding new connections in other areas.

bar coding
catscans
satellite dishes
CDROM
microwaves
fiber optics
nanotechnology
flat panel displays

fuel cells
optoelectronics
digital electronics
smart manufacturing
super materials
diamond thin films
fuzzy logic

See Appendix A on future trends for a fairly complete listing of new technologies that will impact our future.

## 5. New product failures, mistakes and accidents.

Did you know that an airplane is on the wrong course 98% of the time? This is the epitome of learning from mistakes. If the plane just accepted all its mistakes without making corrections then flying would be a pretty hairy situation. And much of our creative thinking also comes from learning from our mistakes.

*Silly Putty* was initially supposed to be General Electric's rubber substitute. As a rubber substitute it was a failure but the chemical engineer that discovered it threw it on the counter and noticed something rather different. It had a very good bounce. Nobody was particularly interested until, years later, a marketing consultant got hold of it, coined it "silly putty", and created a hit. By now you are probably sick of hearing about the glue created by *3M* that didn't work too well. This probable failure, of course, became *Post It* brand products. What if its inventor had thought of it as just another failure and moved on? Once thing for sure - you wouldn't be reading this book since it took about ¼ of the earth's supply of *post-its* to capture all the ideas in it. I heated my house for a full winter on the expelled *post-its* that formed the ides contained here.

A team of scientists from Australia and Canada was trying to develop a chemical that would promote flowering without inducing the body of a plant to grow when they discovered a gibberellin by-product that profoundly suppresses plant growth. This mistake created a new family of products for inhibiting the growth of grass.

Charles Goodyear, an impoverished store clerk, came upon the secret of vulcanization when he accidentally left a sample of rubber and sulfur on a hot stove and charred it. When he picked it up he found a substance that was hard, but pliable and heat resistant. He had discovered the vulcanization process and this discovery led to the establishment of America's rubber industry.

Nitrous oxide gas was used for amusement in the 1800s. In one instance, a demonstrator was calling for volunteers to inhale the gas. One volunteer, who did become violent, scuffled with some people and tripped and fell. The impact sobered him and he took his place beside his friend, a dentist. Soon someone noticed a pool of blood and realized that he had received a rather deep cut from the scuffle. He felt no pain until the gas wore off and his dentist friend saw some immediate possibilities in his field. Anesthesia in operations became a reality.

In 1879 an absent-minded workman left a stirring machine running during the lunch hour and it whipped so much air into the batch of soap that the makers, Proctor and Gamble, first considered throwing it out. But they hated to waste that entire product, so they processed it and sold it. Much to their surprise, they began getting letters from a number of buyers asking for more of the miraculous floating soap.

The process for making Corn and Wheat Flakes came from accidentally leaving some cooked wheat untended for more than a day. When it was run through their rollers they were pleasantly surprised to find it came out flaked instead of in a flat sheet.

Teflon is one of the most famous accidental discoveries. Roy Plunkett, a chemist for E.I. duPont de Numours and Company was actually trying to invent a new type of Freon, a class of compounds that in the 30's were proving to be immensely useful in refrigerators and air conditioners. In their experiment one of the gaseous materials they were producing decided to polymerize. Instead of the containers yielding a good supply of the compound they needed, they contained rather curious flecks of white powder. Fortunately he had the insight to examine this material a little more closely.

Sir Alexander Fleming accidentally dropped some bread mold into a culture of bacteria, contaminating the mixture. Cursing his luck, he looked at the Petri dish under the microscope anyway, and saw within the sea of bacteria islands of clear regions. Fleming had discovered that the mold prevented bacterial growth. The mold was penicillin. A stoke of luck, but Fleming was ready for it.

The original *Slinky*, which entertained children and adults for more than 55 years, was conceived when a tumbling torsion coil accidentally fell from a shelf and sprang to life in the office of inventor Richard James. Fourteen million were sold in its first decade!

Chuck Mellon from Fresno was tossed from his motorbike on an icy mountain trail and tore his sweatshirt. Later, when he put the sweatshirt back on, his thumb poked through a hole in the sleeve accidentally pulling the sleeve down over his hand. That's when the idea struck him for a new type of sweatshirt – one with sleeves that extend over most of the hand and have thumbholes but are fingerless, so they can be rolled back into a normal cuff. Their company, *Handcuff Sweatshirts*, has been doing very well.

And finally, *Scotchguard* was the result of an accidental spill in a laboratory. It was later discovered that the fabric that had received the spill was resistant to soiling.

So the next time you rub up against a failure you should be asking yourself, "In what ways might I put this failure to use?"

## 6. Interesting combinations.

Ideas often emerge from combining various products, operations, or functions. Combining skiing and tobogganing created *sit-down skiing* that is done on a toboggan-like sled with small skis. A new sport is born and new possibilities are triggered for the physically challenged who want to ski. Combining the ski with the boot has resulted in a new ski boot, the *Sled Dog*, which has the skis built right into it. A combination of a *Walk-Man* and sunglasses once created a new product which had the speakers an integral part of the mounting system. Combining the functions of fax, print, and copy has opened up new ways to create multi-function products that take advantage of common engines. And, combining a watch with a radio receiver has produced a watch that can update itself as to its current time zone by analyzing the *fingerprint* of radio frequencies being received.

In a conference of futurists one of the speakers was suggesting the possibility of combining food and pharmaceuticals to produce products in the future she calls *foodaceuticals*. The idea of *edible* vaccines may not be that far away since there is currently research going on using the tools of bioengineering to transform ordinary fruits and vegetables into cargo vessels that will carry life-saving vaccines.

Why can't cellular phones revert to being cordless phones when you pull into your driveway? Think of all the possibilities! It's been said that we never create anything new - we simply make different combinations of things and ideas that currently exist. Keep that thought in mind as you look for ideas that will take you and your company into the future. Everything is already there -

it's just waiting to be re-configured. Are there items or functions in your situation that can be combined to give you competitive advantage?

## 7. A need derived from a current event of high interest.

What are the hot topics or problems of today? By simply reading periodicals and surfing the internet you can keep track of these items and many of them will provide some wonderful new opportunities. Keep a list of current events and ask yourself from time to time what possible connections they might have to new ideas we could use in our business.

## 8. Results of Serendipity.

James Watt is said to have started the industrial revolution with his invention of the steam engine. The idea for his invention came rather serendipitously by observing steam escaping from a teakettle. So you might say that the industrial revolution is a result of serendipity.

Leonardo da Vinci got the idea of sound *waves* after observing that a rock thrown into a pond created waves of water.

Philo Farnsworth had the inspiration that led to television while sitting on a hillside in Idaho. The neat rows of hay in a nearby farm gave him the idea of creating a picture on a cathode ray tube out of rows of light and dark dots. Philo realized an electronic beam could scan the picture in horizontal lines, reproducing the image almost instantaneously. He was 14 at the time and presented the concept at a high school science project. He demonstrated the first working model of a television set when he was 21.

Charles H. Townes (Nobel laureate in physics, 1964) said "The laser was born one beautiful morning on a park bench in Washington DC. As I sat in Franklin Square, musing and admiring the azaleas, an idea came to me for a practical way to obtain a very pure form of electromagnetic waves from molecules."

In 1877, while perfecting a device that would record Morse code on waxed paper so that it could later be transmitted at high speed, Thomas Edison discovered that he could capture the sound of music and the human voice as well. To demonstrate his invention, he recited, "Mary had a little lamb" into the speaker and played it back. Alexander Graham Bell was trying to invent something to help his deaf students, based on a telegraph, when he invented to telephone.

In the early 1950s George deMestral went for a walk in the countryside of his native Switzerland. He returned home to find his jacket covered with cockleburs. As he began picking them off, he wondered, "What makes them stick so tenaciously?" His curiosity led him to use a microscope to investigate more carefully. He discovered that cockleburs are covered with hooks, and the hooks had become embedded in the loops of the fabric of his cloth jackets. He wondered if he could turn this nuisance into something useful and the idea for Velcro was born (derived from combining *velvet* and *crochet*).

In the late 1800s Coca-Cola was not yet visualized as a carbonated drink. It was sweet brown syrup, packaged in reused beer bottles. Called an *Intellectual Beverage and Temperance Drink*, druggists in Atlanta would often mix it with tap water to make it go down easier. A customer appeared one morning with a severe hangover and asks if he could have it immediately to relieve his condition. Rather than walk to the back of the store for tap water the druggist mixed it with soda water. The customer really liked it and an idea was born.

L.J.M. Daguerre invented the first successful photographic process in 1883. He prepared plates of highly polished silver-plated copper and exposed them to iodine vapor that produced a thin layer of silver halide on the surface. Exposing these plates produced a faint image that he tried to intensify without success. One day he placed an exposed plate, which had only a faint image, and which he intended to clean and use again, in a cupboard containing various chemicals and a broken thermometer. After several days, Daguerre removed the plate and found, to his amazement, a strong image on its surface. Through the process of elimination he discovered that the mercury vapor had intensified the image and solved his problem.

Colt came up with his idea for a revolver based on the serendipitous observation of the operation of a paddle wheel.

Serendipity often is connected to dreaming. Dreaming is a great source of ideas and very few people take advantage of this fact. Friedrich August von Kekule (Why couldn't I have been born with a name like that?) had a dream of whirling snakes which allowed him the breakthrough he needed to discover the structure of benzene, an organic chemical compound made up of a ring of carbon atoms. After this he suggested that his associates should start learning to dream.

And finally, the paper industry was born when an eighteenth century French scientist, Rene-Antoine Ferchault de Reaumur, took a walk in the woods. He observed how wasps made paper nests by chewing dry wood, shingles, boards, and fence posts and mixing it with its natural body fluids to form a paste that is spread in dry layers. He wondered why we humans couldn't do this and the questions he raised triggered the start of an industry and products we couldn't imagine being without.

Serendipity is a bit on the *iffy* side. Perhaps you don't have to wait for it to happen. Look for ways to speed up serendipity. Many of the techniques I'll be sharing with you in upcoming chapters will do just that. Keep on reading. I hope you're having as much fun as I am.

## 9. Combining a traditional functionality with a new idea or technology - breaking the rules and assumptions.

There are many things in life that go unchanged for years and years. The nail was invented hundreds of years ago and, although there have been a few enhancements, it's basically unchanged in its form. Along comes an inventor with an idea that a star shaped cross section might have many advantages. Wouldn't you like to have a patent on a better nail? The tennis racquet had the same handle design for years since the sport began until someone came along and wondered why an octagonal shape might be used instead of a hexagonal.

How many engines does a car have? The answer, of course, is one. But Audi challenged this rule and came up with a car with a gas engine in front and an electric one in the rear. Just think of the possibilities with a simple shift in the rules. We've always assumed that there should be one spark plug per cylinder. Mazda is working on breaking this rule by using 3 or 4 per cylinder. This allows combustion to start at the sides and spread to the middle and may result in some quantum leaps in efficiency. Are there any simple rules you can break today?

Who would ever think of a high technology toilet? There are only a few things we can do to a toilet aren't there? Change its shape or its color or upgrade the flushing system. Somebody should have told that to the Japanese. They are creating a whole new line of these that are loaded with technology in the form of biosensors, microprocessors, and other things that should have no place in the lowly commode. Who said the Japanese people aren't creative?

How many poor, lowly, neglected things can you think of that are easy targets for some new thinking? Start by identifying all the things you can think of that haven't been changed since you were knee high to a grasshopper.

## 10.    Observations from nature applied to problems.

We've seen the impact that wasps have had on creating the paper industry. Nature has a way of demonstrating some wonderful ideas. Not matter what your problem or opportunity you can ask for examples from nature and always be insured of coming up with new ideas. Here's a question for you. What marvel of chemical engineering makes all the following products?

1. Five-millisecond epoxy glue.
2. A water-soluble material produced in water.
3. A flexible, but inelastic fiber.
4. Another fiber stronger than nylon fishing line and ten times tougher than Kevlar which is 1/1000 the thickness of a nickel and can support an apple.

The answer is a spider. This is just one example of many marvels of nature that we need to learn from.

Have you ever known a cat that has had difficulty sleeping? A chemist at Scripps Research Institute in La Jolla, California used what he called the "Willie Sutton logic of natural products" to find naturally produced substances to coax the brain to sleep.

Willie Sutton, of course, is the bank robber who was asked why he robs banks. His answer was, "Because that's where the money is". Careful studies revealed a "sleep molecule", a very costly compound manufactured by the cat's body to induce sleep. Could cats eventually become sleeping pill manufacturers? Why use examples from nature as triggers for new thinking? Because that's where the answers often lie.

Photographers attempted using infrared film to take pictures of polar bears for counting because warm bodies stand out from their surroundings in infrared images. Surprisingly, the photos returned from the developer were blank. The animal is basically invisible to the best cameras because so little heat escapes through their fur. Think of the possible uses for the military including warm soldiers and tanks that could not be seen with infrared spotting devices. Further studies of this hair found that it is a good transmitter of ultraviolet light and scientists are in the process of studying the hair for clues about how to construct ultraviolet lasers used for delicate theory.

There is a fish called a *ramora* that attaches itself to a shark and goes along for the ride (personally, I think I'd attach myself to something else). When some cameramen saw this they immediately got the idea for designing the *Critter Cam* based on what they saw. And here's another fish story. The *Green Sunfish*, a freshwater fish native to the Northeast can spot its prey and predators in murky, algae-filled waters. The sunfish, unlike humans can apparently see polarized light. This fact has lead engineers to the exploration of the fish's retinal calls and some possible breakthroughs in techniques for creating vision in foggy situations.

There has long been a fascination with the snake as a symbol of healing. It has recently been discovered that the proteins found in the venom of the Brazilian pit viper can have a positive impact on the lowering of blood pressure. And the health store shelves are packed with dozens of miracle cures such as *Pycnogenol* from natural origins.

A new area of research called biomimetics focuses on the study of the structure and function of biological substances as models for material design and manufacturing. From this field have come new ideas such as byssal threads from mussels for repairing human tendons and ligaments. Biomimetics, or biological mimicking, has attracted researchers from fields as seemingly unconnected as materials science, molecular biology, engineering, biochemistry, mathematics, and physics. These researchers all share a deep fascination with the precision, elegance, and ingenuity of biological systems and realize that nature has had several billion years of R&D that we can learn from. We need to learn why abalone shells are so hard and why some of the strongest glue ever produced comes from barnacles.

**11. A technology breakthrough or shift that makes impossibilities possible.**

How about some electricity-generating roof shingles? As breakthroughs in the reliability and efficiency of photovoltaic panels are achieved, we get closer to the possibility of electricity generating roof shingles. As each technology reaches a breakthrough stage in its development hundreds of opportunities unfold. Companies that want to be on the cutting edge of their business must track technologies; even the ones they think will have no impact.

How about speakers the size of *Oreo Cookies*? New technological breakthroughs in sound from crystals are revolutionizing the speaker industry, an industry that had relied upon electrical signals vibrating diagrams since 1925.

One of the biggest breakthroughs that triggered a landslide of new opportunities was an invention by Tim Bernes-Lee. He invented a scheme for linking a document of any kind stored on any computer connected to the Internet. Dubbed the *Universal Resource Locator*, or URL, this innovation gave everything on the Internet its own unique address. Type a URL into a special program called a web browser, and the program would go out to the Internet, fetch the information, and display it on your computer screen. Sounds pretty simple, doesn't it? But Bernes-Lee's invention of the URL made possible the sci-fi vision of having the world's information at the click of a button.

Some might say that all new inventions were impossible at one time. Any time there is a technology breakthrough there is the possibility of a landslide of new connecting ideas. And, remember, these technologies don't necessarily have to be closely connected to what you are working on.

## 12. The need to get rid of things we have in excess.

The disposal of truck and car tires has long posed a gigantic problem in our society. Recently a novel approach that strangely connects the problem to its root source uses this ground-up rubber to build noise barriers along main highways. Ground-up rubber crumbs are used to fill the fiberglass walls and each mile uses somewhere around 20,000 tires. This process far exceeds other walls in effectiveness to reduce sound while reducing the massive landfills of tires.

A rather novel approach of getting rid of manure is the popular Zoo Doos. These are small sculptures of animals designed for gardens and made from compressed manure. If someone can make a product out of manure then there must be ways to turn all trash into cash.

There is a vine called kudzu in the southeastern United States that overruns fields, covers buildings, and smothers other vegetation. An enterprising seventh grader decided to make paper out of kudzu - and was successful. After learning about it, some Georgia Tech students took some vines from an Atlanta field, chopped them into small pieces, and threw them into a pressure cooker with water and some chemicals. They cooked it, broke it down by hand, pressed it into sheets, and set it out to dry. Along came Kudzu paper. The process is currently under refinement.

## 13. Things that don't make sense to you – wandering and wondering.

Several years ago I was teaching a group of assemblers the techniques of creative thinking. For some reason I gave them a long break and asked them to wander around a bit and look at things they normally don't look at, and to wonder about what they saw. When they returned to the session I was shocked by the new, creative input. I've tried this wandering and wondering approach often since then - always with great results. Some of us are under the misguided assumption that we are too smart to wonder. They pay me all those bucks because I'm supposed to know things, not wonder about them. Einstein spent a lot of time wondering - and he was no dummy. So next time you are doing something where your mind is on cruise control, take some time to let your mind wander a little farther away, follow it around, and wonder about what you might change.

For example, the last time I was gassing up my car, my mind wandered to the question, "Why can't I have a digital readout on the handle so I wouldn't have to turn and face the pump to see where I was?" And, while doing my laundry, I wondered why I couldn't have a marker that helped me match up socks so that missing ones could find their partners.

## 14. Impossibilities

I recently got a fortune cookie with a meal that read, "All great accomplishments were once considered impossible". Maybe we should consider the ideas contained in fortune cookies more often. A good start to creating breakthrough in any area is to ask what's impossible to do.

What's impossible to do in your life and your work right now? Stop reading and tackle this question. The answers to it will yield all sorts of new possibilities.

## 15. Creating the exact opposite of everything people wanted the day before.

A recent Toshiba add said, "Innovation is easy. You just create the exact opposite of what everyone wanted yesterday". Most car companies have always thought that locking the steering was the answer to car theft. This was done through factory installation or by use a *club*. The opposite is having a steering wheel that unlocks without the key so it just spins free. The British are developing this concept now.

As financial institutions gear up to tap into the growing older populations lenders are beginning to write more and more *reverse* mortgages. A *reverse* mortgage is a loan against a home's equity with a twist: the lending institution makes monthly payments to the borrower, who usually must be at least 62. When the homeowner sells, moves, or dies the loan becomes due and the borrowed money plus interest is paid from the proceeds of the house.

The typical process for building a house is to build from the bottom up. A Japanese homebuilder claims that going from the top down is quicker, cheaper, and safer for the workers. The house is built at ground level starting with the top and then jacked up so that the next level is at the ground floor working level.

And a company called Viad Corporation is anchored in a leading edge business philosophy called "narrowcasting." Defined as the practice of aiming a program or service at a specific audience or sales market, they are the first to pioneer its unique application as a strategy for future growth. While the rest of the world thinks *broadcasting*, this little company may be carving out a comfortable niche for themselves by thinking opposite.

Organizations that rely on customer focus groups as the gospel of what they should produce may be headed for trouble. Some of the most unique and successful products are ones that are different and most customers are using their patterns of thinking from the past in developing stated desires for the future.

Think of some things that are exact opposites of what you or your customers expect and see what novel new ideas come to mind.

## 16. Recreating something that has been lost.

One of my great passions is the collecting of music, particularly jazz and classical. Compact discs created a new media that opened up new possibilities to re-create some great music from the past. Jazz has many great new artists but the major growth here seems to be in the developing of catalogue of historic music that is surprising high quality. I believe that there will be a growing desire for nostalgic trips to the past in many different areas. This will be driven by the tremendous surge of boomers. This group will have money to spend and many of them will not have a tremendous desire to go forward into new technologies.

How might you re-create some things that have been lost in your product or service area? How might you make your product appeal to the sense of nostalgia in your customers?

## 17. Putting more fun into something.

The older I get the more I dislike doing anything that isn't fun. I'm convinced I'm not alone in this and that one great source of new ideas comes from asking how to make our products and services more fun. How can driving be more fun? How can the Registry of Motor Vehicles be more fun? How can work be more fun? There is virtually nothing that can't benefit from raising its fun quotient.

## 18. From the information hidden within an existing product or service

Stan Davis in his book, *2020 Vision*, suggests the 80-20 rule. By 2020, 80% of all business profits will come from that part of the enterprise built around the information business. There are some interesting examples of the tremendous value of the information that exists within the domain of current business. *TV Guide* is said to be worth more than any of the networks. The *Sabre System* of airline reservations is said to be valued at more than American Airlines, their creator. A key question then might be "What products and services might be derived from the information contained within my current product line"?

New information technologies and capabilities are opening up possibilities that never existed before. A nagging problem in the imaging business has long been related to the information within the images and there weren't many answers until the digital domain appeared. The cataloging and manipulation of the information regarding images will create some great new possibilities in the future.

There is also an intriguing law regarding information that may have some interesting implications. If I sell you a pen, you end up with the pen and I end up with the money. If I sell you information, you end up with the information. I end up with the money, but I also still have the information. Play with this a bit if you have a situation where information may be a key area for product ideas. Does the fact that you can sell something but still have it open any interesting doors?

## 19. Listening to questions from people who don't know as much as you do.

Edward Land was taking pictures of his family while on a vacation trip in the southwest. His young daughter asked, "Why do we have to wait to see the pictures?" and Land thought to himself "good question" sketched out some ideas and tried them after he returned to his lab in Boston. The Polaroid camera and the science of instant photography appeared soon thereafter.

## So What?

So, what might we learn from all this? Now that you know how ideas are born what would you change in your own situation? Could you create forced serendipity? Are there ways you could create more time for wondering, getting outrageous, making more

66

mistakes, playing with opposites, cross fertilizing, combining technologies, and incubating of ideas? The next two chapters will give you some great techniques for doing some of these things.

Generating new ideas for business is like digging clams. If you keep going to the same place, pretty soon you won't be finding any clams. You need to always be thinking about how to get off the beaten path. A quotation from Tao Te Ching by Lao Tsu would be appropriate for bringing closure to this chapter:

> Thirty spokes share the wheel's hub;
> It is the center hole that makes it useful.
> Shape clay into a vessel;
> It is the space within that makes it useful.
> Cut doors and windows for a room;
> It is the holes that make it useful.
> Therefore, profit comes from what is there;
> Usefulness from what is not there.

# Chapter 3

# A Left Brain Look at the Right Brain

# A Creative Thinking Process Overview

The purpose of this chapter is to take a somewhat rational look at various techniques for enhancing the ideation process. The so-called *brainstorming* process has been around for a long time and often used with marginal effectiveness. One reason is that those who use it fail to prepare the participants and get them into the right frame of thinking. Expecting people to brainstorm without some preparation is like expecting them to jump out of bed and run a marathon. They need to understand, and believe the guidelines to be followed in the process.

The content of the group is very important. My experience is that there is a tendency to load brainstorming groups with so called experts on the subject matter. The problem with that is that they all tend to know too much and that can sometimes get in the way. They may have difficulty overcoming their thinking paradigms. I've always found it useful to toss in a few folks from totally different backgrounds that had little or no knowledge of the subject matter. I've sometimes thrown in some who had expertise in entirely different areas.

Here are the guidelines I have used up front with groups.

## Guidelines for Ideation

- You are an incredibly creative person as are all the others here.
- You can't make any mistakes or say anything wrong. Don't be afraid to verbalize ideas that are not yet well thought out. Planting "idea seeds" is a great way to kick up thinking.
- Everything anyone else says is a revelation and a great building block for a new idea in your own mind.
- Silly, ridiculous, outrageous, and childlike are desirable frames of mind.

- Everything is connected and everything can be expanded.
- If at first you don't succeed, give up. Take a break and let the ideas marinate for a while.
- Have fun. There will be no longer than a 15-minute stretch without some laughter.

I also suggest they practice what I call ***pinball thinking***. The idea is to keep thoughts suspended like pin balls as long as you can while interacting with as many other things as possible to develop new thoughts.

In a group setting it's almost always a good idea to start off with a warm-up session to help them practice the use of the guidelines. This is like stretching the muscles before exercise and it really works. In Chapter 4 there are numerous warm-ups. Don't spend too much time here - just enough to get the group cooking. If the thinking becomes rigid at any point in time it may be a good idea to re-visit the warm-ups. With some groups it may be a good idea to re-visit the warm-up every hour or so just to get the thinking juices reflowing.

Ideas need to be captured. If you don't capture them somehow, then you will most likely lose them. You may use a scribe for capturing the ideas on chart paper (which may significantly slow down the ideating process), capture them on a laptop or IPad (with projector if possible), or use post-it notes. Post-its are my favorite because it shares the load and doesn't let anything get lost in a scribe's translation. The idea originator explains his or her idea and then hangs it up. The ideas can later be arranged in categories and processed.

The other thing to understand about the ideation process is the nature of its successive stages. Many so-called brainstorming sessions are carried out only to the first stage. "Let's write down

71

all the ideas we can think of." The problem here is that you'll get only those ideas that are currently close to the surface (the low hanging fruit). To really tap the potential of the ideation process you need to take it several levels beyond this using various **braintickling** techniques. The various ideation stages are:

*Idea Purging* – Get out those initial reactions to the problem or opportunity. If these are not purged they might block out new and different thinking. This is not to say that some of these initial thoughts aren't valuable because there very well might be some great ideas in the initial purge. Get them out but don't discount them.

*Initial Braintickler* – Use an idea stimulating technique that will give the *ideators* a chance to look at the problem or opportunity in a different way and also build on the initial idea purge.

*Kicked Up Braintickler* – Use a technique that builds on where they are right now and takes them to a totally new place in their thinking.

*Excursion* - Take a trip away from the problem or opportunity to give them an opportunity to re-boot their thinking. When you are far enough away from the initial thinking begin creating force fits back to the problem or opportunity.

*Visit Crazy Land* – You'll never explore all the opportunities unless you visit the absurd – those things that are impossible and totally ridiculous. This will create the stretch you need to open up another wave of possibilities.

*Cool Down* – This gives you the chance to take a look at what you have and gather any new thoughts and ideas that are triggered by what you see.

*Post Brainstorming Incubation Time* – Some of the best ideas come after the session while incubating in the minds of the participants. If possible find some way to get that input from them.

I put these techniques into eight categories for teaching purposes but there is a good deal of crossover between the categories. My personal file of techniques numbers well into the hundreds and I'll be telling you about many of them in the next few chapters. I suggest you take whatever creative license you'd like to embellish these techniques. There is nothing that says you must stick to the process exactly how it's described. And, if you find something that really works well for you, just go for it.

The categories are:

- Mind stretchers
- Word play
- Wandering and Excursions
- Viewpoint shifts
- Metaphors and Analogies
- Brainwriting

## Mind Stretchers

I sometimes refer to this as *Mental Bunge Jumping*. This category consists of techniques designed to stretch you well beyond what you presently think is possible. They really get you into the *creative zone* where it's okay to fantasize, get totally outrageous, and think and do silly things. Going to the creative zone involves leaving the reality zone and some people feel uncomfortable doing this. But that's exactly why you want to do this. You want to get people out of their comfort zones even if it's a little painful for them at first. They may ultimately love you for it!

I've probably said this before but I just can't stress it enough. Going to a places that are well beyond what you've ever imagined and then coming back to reality puts you at a very different spot than pushing yourself forward from reality. It's also a lot more fun. So you have two choices of identifying new opportunities or solving a problem:

> Carry out an ideation session to generate new ideas based on our current thinking which will take you to a certain end result or take a mental bungee jump to a certain fantasy land of possibilities and work back to a point where you may be able to make this happen. The second process will likely lead to some much more interesting possibilities.

Which end result would you rather have? Stretching your thinking into fantasyland and then coming back to reality can be much more productive and a lot more exciting. On one hand you are asking how we might do something based on our view of what is possible right now. On the other, you are creating possibilities where they never before existed

An interesting metaphor to describe how new ideas are generated in the process of stretching is the development of muscles from exercise. Bringing them to the point where the fiber is about to fracture develops muscles. Just before fracture the nerves send out a message to strengthen the muscle and, as this is repeatedly done, new muscle is formed. Why shouldn't brain muscles follow the same general rule?

Here are a few techniques that fall into this category.

**Braintickler #1 Fantasizing**

The keywords here are, "I wish _____," and, "What if
_____?" Whatever your problem or opportunity is you can fill in
the blanks here with anything you want. If you're trying to design
a safer light posts along the highway one of your "What ifs?"
might be, "What if we could have posts that just disappear when
hit?" A group actually did that once and was able to create a post
that disappeared when hit. Okay, it didn't really disappear - it just
*kind of* disappeared. They designed one that fractured without
doing a great deal of damage to the vehicle and flipped itself over
the car. Do you see what this question was able to do in this case?
It got them to the point of stating something that was *impossible*
and they were able to bring it back to the point that it was *kind of
possible*.

As an example let's assume you are looking for new ideas for a
camera. Here are just a few things that might result from our
fantasizing questions.

I wish I could take a picture of what I'm thinking.
I wish I had my camera at all times.
I wish I could get a perfect picture every time.
What if the camera were a part of my body?
What if my camera told me when there was a good picture
opportunity?
What if my picture was instantly transferred to my friends and
family?
What if my pictures were automatically put into the appropriate
albums?

Each of these triggers a new set of possibilities. The key is to pick some and expand on ways to make the fantasies come true.

**Braintickler #2 - Crazy Criteria**

This is particularly good for developing new product enhancements and ideas but could be used for about anything. I want to thank my friend and creative hero, Sid Shore, for this one. It's based on the thought that the end results of something we design is determined by the criteria in our minds as we proceed with the project. If we have some run of the mill criteria the chances are we'll end up with a run of the mill end result. For example, if you're designing a car the chances are that you'll be driven by the following criteria:

comfort
economy
safety
attractiveness
performance
reliability
cost

There's certainly nothing wrong with this criteria but it is a little on the dull side. Let's look at some crazy criteria. I want a car that:

scratches my back when I drive
floats on water
expands and contracts
folds up into a briefcase
does my lawn
cooks my meals
serves as my coffin

reproduces itself
becomes an added room for my house
pilots itself
flies
pays my bills

In a group session expect a lot of wild criteria and keep pushing for even wilder ones. From this list you can take off in all directions using the criteria as springboards for generating new, crazy ideas. For example, in what ways might we create a car that expands and contracts? How might we build on the thought that a car could become a room in our house? At some point you can begin to bring it on home to reality, by taking a look at some of the crazy ideas that have some possibility, and identifying how you might make then come true.

## Braintickler #3 - Rule Busting

Every problem or opportunity we work on has some rules attached. Other words for rules are paradigms, assumptions, impossibilities, guidelines, patterns, regulations, and accepted behaviors. This mind stretcher deliberately tries to break all these rules. The first step is to identify what the rules are and this is not as easy as it sounds because we often take them for granted and often don't even know they exist.

Identify a problem or opportunity. As our example let's consider how we might motivate people in the workplace.

What are the rules (both stated and un-stated) associated with this problem or opportunity?

>People come to work each day.
>Everyone has a particular job to do.

Money is their reward.

What are the assumptions we make regarding the problem?

> Work is very serious.
> People are excited about their work.
> People are not naturally highly motivated.

What is impossible to do today in the areas associated with the opportunity that, if they were possible, would change the game?

> People can't just do what turns them on in a work environment.
> Everyone can't be working at different times.
> Everyone must be rewarded in the same way.

What are the accepted behaviors for those involved in all areas of the problem?

> Perform according to your job descriptions.
> Do your job and don't ask questions.
> Be in your workplace at all times.

Now go back through these observations and generate as many statements as you can that break the rules. Make sure they really break the rules - we're talking a major fracture, not just a bruise. Every time you make a rule breaking statement you should ask, "How might I break this some more?"

> People can come to work anytime they want.
> People can work from their homes.
> Each person identifies his or her own rewards.
> People can pick what job turns them on each day.

Pick some of the more interesting statements from the previous step and bring them back to reality. Ask:

Is it okay to break this rule? If not, why not?
How might we break it in a way that's possible?
What are some alternatives to breaking it?
What other possibilities exist related to this breakage?

## Braintickler #4 - Successive stages of outrageousness

For those who thrive in a group on out-doing each other this technique is heaven sent (only kidding). The idea here is to have someone suggest an outrageous (or mildly outrageous) and identify all the ways to make it more and more outrageous. As a matter of fact, maybe you don't even need to start with outrageous. Just follow the normal brainstorming process and take a detour into insanity for each idea that comes up. By the way, this is a great deal of fun too. Let's see if I can map out the process.

State the problem or opportunity.

Each person generates as many ideas as they can.

Each person in the group states an idea that rather excites them.

The group begins to raise the level of outrageousness by asking successively: How can this idea be made more outrageous? Take it to the limit. The last idea in this series should be the epitome of total ridiculousness.

Start with another person's idea and raise its level of outrageousness and continue as before.

79

End the exercise when all participants are either asleep or nearly brain dead.

## Braintickler #5 – Getting fired

Most of us try to keep our thinking on the straight and narrow most of the time because we like the idea of keeping our job. After all, suggesting some really weird possibilities could just put you on the short list in the eyes of your boss. So let's just change the goals of your group a little. Their goal is to suggest enough things that are so stupid, and so outrageous that it will get them fired. Let's really see if we can bring this outfit down! You could build a veritable contest to see who can get fired first by suggesting the greatest number of totally ridiculous ideas. Warning – make sure this is truly a safe situation for people. Remember that the object is to get people to really stretch their thinking to places it's never been so that you can come back to possibilities that you can make happen. This process can be a lot of fun. When's the last time you had a chance to get fired at work and could let it all out like this?

# Word Play

It's amazing how many ideas can be derived from ideas built on the words. This could be words within problem or opportunity statements, various derivatives of these words, or just words out of the blue. This series of techniques involves word associations and excursions from words collected from a variety of sources.

## Braintickler #6 - Word Blenders

One of the most successful techniques I've used in past ideation sessions involves various techniques using random words. Just pick words out of a dictionary, magazines, or other handy sources. They don't need to have any particular connection to your problem. As a matter of fact, the less connected ones are often better idea stimulators. Write these words on chart paper or, even better, on small pieces of paper. If they are on small pieces of paper mix them up and put them in a container. Everyone in the group then randomly picks 3 or so words and uses these words as idea stimulators. What does the word make you think of? If you combine the words in various ways what does that make you think of? What possibilities do these new thoughts trigger? Pass the words around within the group for further stimulation or take some new ones from the blender. Substitute words in the problem statement with some of your new words. Think of the opposites or of synonyms of the words and identify new thoughts that are triggered. Twist, bend, stretch, compress, and alter these words any way you see fit. If you torture them enough they will confess to their hidden secrets.

## Braintickler#7 – Rhyming

I first saw this technique used at a conference on creative techniques. For the life of me I can't remember who the originator was or I would give credit. If you were the originator, let me know and I'll give you my first born great grand child. It involves taking two or three words from the problem statement and then creating lists of rhyming words from each of them. When you can't think of a rhyming word then create a bridge of some sort to another series (a similar item, reversal, opposite, backwards etc.). It's a quick, fun way to generate a bunch of words that have an interesting connection to your base problem. It's harder to explain than it is to do so here's an example.

Problem: In what ways might we really *turn* people on in their *jobs*?

Turn – burn – fern – learn – teach (reversal) – beach – peach – breach - reach
Jobs – mobs – slobs – blobs – globs – clogs – frogs – smog – smoke (similar) – poke – woke

You may wonder what this can all have to do with turning someone on in their job. Well, that's what creativity is all about. These words take us off into another direction, another mindset. Now the task is to see if we can force fit them back to our problem. What new thoughts are stimulated by peaches, frogs, blobs, and poking?

**Braintickler #8 – First Thoughts**

This technique generates several banks of words based on what you first think of when you hear key words in the problem or opportunity statement. It has the ability to generate many words quickly that, for some strange reason, have creative connections to the base statement. Take a key word from the statement and ask everyone what other word first comes to mind. Then take one of the most intriguing of these words, and ask the same question. Repeat it again with a new, intriguing word from the new list. I find it most useful to chart these words in columns on a chart pad. The next step is to have each person select 3-4 words from these new lists and create new ideas based on thoughts triggered by them.

Let's say that the word, *organize*, was a keyword in the problem statement. Here's how the generation of word might unfold (bold words are the selected ones for generating new first thoughts). What does organize make you think of?

82

| Crime | Teachers | **Diapers** |
|-------|----------|-------------|
| Accountants | Dictionaries | Learning |
| Desks | Phone books | Small |
| Files | **Children** | Expensive |
| Neat | Schoolrooms | Energized |
| Teamwork | IPads | Screaming |
| **Alphabetic** | Encyclopedias | Hungry |
| | | |
| | Avoid | Pins |
| Smelly | **Impenetrable** | Pales |
| Disposable | White | |

Now you have some new words that have an interesting link to the problem but are far enough away to create some new ideas.

**Braintickler #9 – Stimulus analysis approach**

The Battelle Institute developed this technique and I've found it particularly useful for creating new thinking for hardware type problems. It uses a series of stimulus words developed by the group and uses the characteristics of these as stepping stones to form ideas. Let's look at an example problem.

How might we warn press operators when their hands are in danger of being caught as the press closes?

Have the group develop a list on 10 concrete items that are unrelated to the problem. For example:

| Desk | Television |
|------|-----------|
| Table Lamp | Motorcycle |
| Lawn Mower | Restaurant |
| Football team | Refrigerator |

Movie Theater                    Hotel

Select one of the terms and have the group break it down into its
descriptive characteristics (structures, principles, and specific
details). Breaking the lamp down into characteristic might include:

- ❑ Uses electricity
- ❑ Emits light
- ❑ Generates heat
- ❑ Clicks when turned on

The group then analyzes each of these characteristics one by one to
identify possible solutions to the original problem.

- ❑ Apply a mild shock to operator as a warning.
- ❑ Use a photoelectric cell to trip switch.
- ❑ Use temperature-sensing cell to detect heat from hands.
- ❑ Have press emit a loud clicking sound at a certain point.

After enough creative ideas are generated, select a new stimulus
and repeat the process. Do this for all ten items identified.

**Braintickler #10 – Changing the Verbs**

A very simple method for stimulating ideas is to look at the key
Verbs in the problem statement and develop as many similar
words as you can for these. For example, assume the group was
working on the problem:

In what ways might we better distribute our product?

The group might take a closer look at the word *distribute*. Some
words that convey the same meaning might include, give away,

84

deal, hand out, disperse, dispense, deliver, bestow, administer, circulate, etc. These new verbs could then be used as stepping stones for new ideas. Free association or analogies formed on these new words could add some new directions to their ideas.

# Wandering and Excursions

Much creative thinking comes when we get as far away from our problem as possible and look for connections well outside the current scope of things. Some of these techniques take us on physical excursions and some on mental ones. Mental excursions can be done using pictures, catalogues, magazines, or fantasy trips. Physical excursions can be as simple as a walk in the woods or through a store.

### Braintickler #11 - Catalogues and maga*zines*

The use of catalogues or magazines has the power to trigger some really different thinking. Keep a good inventory of these to use in ideation sessions because they never fail to stimulate new ideas. The biggest problem is to keep people out of the shopping mode. Get as creative as you want in terms of the process used. Here are a couple of ways I've use catalogues and magazines.

Hand out catalogues randomly to everyone in the group. Ask people to randomly open their catalogues to a page and tell you something they see. Make sure they understand that these don't have to have an immediate connection to the problem or opportunity being worked on. Otherwise they will be screening the trigger words before they verbalize them. Write these objects on a piece of chart paper and do it until you have a chart full of objects. Then ask people to write down new ideas for whatever problem you are working on based on these particular objects and the things they make you think of. Repeat this several times with new words as necessary.

Here's a more interactive option that really gets people moving around and is lots of fun. Have people select an intriguing item from their catalogue and write in on a medium size post-it note. This post-it note is then placed on their forehead and everyone walks around to see what others have. Each person writes down one of more new ideas that the items trigger for them as they walk around checking everyone else out. There is something about walking around and staring at people who have sticky notes on their forehead that creates a bit of a different environment and it's a lot of fun to boot. When everyone is finished track all the new ideas and any that build from them.

**Braintickler #12 -   Stimulation**

I find that some of my most creative thinking takes place on road trips. Somehow the stimulus provided from the ever-changing scenery is very powerful. Unfortunately it's a little hard to take a group on a road trip to get them thinking differently. So what you do is to bring the road trip to them. I used a collection of slides with a variety of pictures that have the power to take people on some wonderful trips. It's important to use slides with a wide range of themes and even include some that are perhaps just outright weird. The idea is to look at these pictures for 3-4 minutes each and write down the thoughts that come to your mind. What do these pictures make you think of? Don't worry about defining a clear connection to the problem yet – just write down anything that comes to mind. After looking at several pictures and the noting the thoughts they illicit, have each person spend several minutes identifying new possibilities that connect to the problem or opportunity being worked on. You'll be surprised at the amount, and the creativity of the results.

So you don't happen to have a bunch of hand selected slides for this exercise? Just cut out some picture from some magazines and pass them out to people. Or paste some pictures into catalogues that are several pages long leaving room to jot down ideas and have people pass them around in a group and adding new thoughts as they look at each picture. Or you might want to just have people scan magazines for pictures that evoke new thinking. There's lots of ways to do this but the result is the same. The pictures bring out many new and different ideas.

## Braintickler #13 - Creativity by wandering around

I remember a workshop I was doing some years ago at Kodak where we were teaching operators how to think creatively. We had been working for a long while on various techniques and it was time for a break. It was right about the time when Tom Peters had popularized the words, *managing by wandering around*. I decided to give them a longer than usual break and ask them to wander around and collect new triggers and new ideas for the problem we were working on. I instructed them to go places that weren't normal for them, look in directions they normally didn't look, notice things they normally didn't notice, and not to be afraid to stop and ask people along the way for their ideas. I thought it would be relaxing for them but my expectations of them coming back with some creative new thoughts wasn't that high.

Boy was I wrong! When we all got back together the flow of ideas was like an avalanche! I remember a couple of the students that pretty much spent all their time in the vending machine area using these machines as a trigger for new ideas. And they had some great new ideas. The new ideas that come back from this process are always fresh and different and everyone seems to be re- energized in the creative thinking processes from it. I've done this many times and the experience has always blown me away. I find it helps to give the group a generous amount of time particularly if they are a little worn out to begin with. Also, suggesting some goals as to how many new ideas to bring back helps too.

**Braintickler #14 – Planned Physical excursions**

If the time is available it can be quite effective to build in a planned excursion. This might be a walk in the woods to look for metaphors and triggers from various aspects of nature. Or it might be trips to a variety of retail locations where people could observe a large number of idea triggers. It may even be a show or a movie. The idea as in all excursions is to get people out of their normal thinking boundaries, away from the problem, and into a position where they can discover some new connections. The fact that it is a physical excursion means that they have a chance for physical exercise and that helps the mental process a great deal too.

**Braintickler #15 - Mental metamorphosis**

Albert Einstein was known for taking mental excursions into the problems he was dealing with. He would take a ride on a light wave in his mind and try to identify what was happening. Just think of what you can learn by becoming what you are working on. My first experience with this technique was with a group of engineers that were trying to create new ideas for future automobile HVAC (heating, ventilating, and air conditioning) systems.

I asked them to break down the HVAC systems to 4-5 specific components and assigned small groups to literally become these components. One became the blower system, one became the control system, one became the cooling system, and so forth. Their task was to learn what it's like being that particular component. They were asked the following questions:

♦  What does it feel like being _____?

- What makes you so special?

- What really turns you on?

- What upsets you?

- What would you change if you could?

Each group then shared their results and I summarized some of the main learning points. I might add that there was a lot of laughter and a few engineers that were quite shocked by how much they had learned in the process. A downloading of ideas to explore regarding future HVAC systems followed this.

I suggest doing a mental metamorphosis early in the process because of its ability to get you off to a strong start and give people a very different understanding of the problem. This technique is very effective when used in product design but its options are not limited to that area. You have the ability to become anything you want.

## Viewpoint Shifting

Here the object is simply to become somebody or something else. Trade business cards within your group and become the other person, become your favorite hero, put on the hat of another person, or become the object you're working on.

**Braintickler #16 - Questioning to change viewpoints**

The purpose of this line of questioning is to get the group to look at their problem in a different and unique way. My friend, Sidney Shore, had something he called Creative Action Catalysts which have used successfully a number of times.

C --- Combine (with something else, itself, another problem etc.)
R --- Reverse (upside down, inside out, negative space around etc.)
E --- Enlarge (magnify the problem, or its parts)
A --- Adapt (other similar problems, other ideas suggested etc.)
T --- Tinier (subtract something, condense, make smaller, shorter etc.)
I --- In Place Of (make substitutions, change ingredients etc.)
V --- Viewpoint Change (look at from the eyes of a different person)
I --- In Other Sequence (interchange components)
T --- To Other Uses
Y --- Yes! Yes! (a reminder that anything is possible)

## Braintickler #17 – New thinking hats

In my years as a creative process consultant with Kodak I began a collection of hats representing different people (policeman, fireman, little old ladies, golfers, baseball/football players, chefs, toddlers, armed forces, clowns, Rastafarians, you name it). Sometimes I'd I throw in something other than a hat (apron, skirt, toga etc.). To shift viewpoints I would have people wear these different hats and become the person they represented and generate ideas based on this new viewpoint. Often I would have them switch hats and become another person. This was always a blast and the ideas emerging from this process were always different and exciting.

## Braintickler #18 - My favorite heroes

In this viewpoint shift the idea is to become your favorite hero. Begin by having the group identify a list of their favorite heroes. Then each person can pick a hero and become that person and generate ideas and thoughts as that person might. Ideas coming from this process may be very high quality because these are your heroes talking.

**Braintickler #19 – Become your problem**

Einstein frequently used this process in his thinking and, let's face it, he was no slouch! One of the most interesting viewpoint shifts may be obtained by getting inside your problem and play acting that part. I have orchestrated hundreds of ideation sessions but one of my most memorable was with a major auto company who were trying to create new ideas to enhance their automotive HVAC (heating, ventilating, and air conditioning) systems. I organized the ideation group into various teams representing the major components of this system (controls, fans, supply lines, coils etc). Then I had them each go off and become the system they were representing. I asked them to identify how they felt and the things that bothered them, the things that really turned them on, what they liked and disliked about the other systems, what things they'd like changed and a few other odd questions.

They then came back together and each one told their story while others took notes. That was followed by a general ideation session based on what everyone heard. The result was quite impressive and different! And it was a blast!

**Brainticler #20 Role playing**

If the desire is to improve products or services it may be wise to bring in some of the most important people of all. These are your customers, stockholders, employees, and competition. Role playing these people to find out what they would like to see changed. There are lots of ways to carry out role playing but make sure the process is fun for all involved.

# Metaphors and Analogies

Some of the most powerful creative processes involve the use of metaphors. Asking why an organization is like a plate of spaghetti and meatballs or a compost pile is a creative alternative to starting a conversation on how to improve an organization. It allows you to get into the creative zone without encountering a lot of judgmental behavior. It opens up thinking. Techniques involving metaphorically drawing problems can supply powerful new thinking and create great new visions of what is possible.

**Braintickler #21 – Describing Your Problem or Opportunity using Metaphors**

Use the following list of possibilities to describe your problem or opportunity. Why is my problem or opportunity similar to this item and how does thinking about in these terms help me to create new possibilities?

| | |
|---|---|
| A Mud Slide | An Old Dog |
| Jell-O with Fruit | A Mountain Bike |
| Silly Putty | Jack in the Box |
| The Titanic | A Slinky |
| A Dinosaur | A Rubber Chicken |
| A Forest | Ace Ventura |
| Juggling | General Hospital |
| War | A Cage of Birds |
| A Flower Garden | A Sail Boat |
| An Elephant | Disney Land |
| A Game of Scrabble | Star Trek |
| An Orchestra | A Compost Pile |
| Spaghetti & Meatballs | Various Internal Body Organs |
| An Amoeba | Chinese Finger Puzzles |
| An Ice Cream Sunday | Chicken Soup |
| A Flea Sale | Monopoly |
| A Game of Pool | A Bottle of Whiskey |

Schools of Fish
A Grasshopper
Trivial Pursuit
A Tool Box
A Stir Fry
A Game of Twister
A Whack-A-Mole Game
The Senate and the House
A Shopping Mall
The Circus
A Drive-in Movie
A Spider Web

A Tree
A Hard Drive
Buffalo Chips
Earth Worms
A Pogo Stick
Raising Children
Tooth Plaque
A Can of Sardines
Panty Hose
A TV Sitcom
Crazy Glue

If you can actually have the object there it becomes even more stimulating. However, I wouldn't suggest earthworms, cow chips,

or compost piles. It could get a little messy.

**Braintickler #22 – Analogies to unrelated fields**

Analogies from other unrelated provide good stepping stones for new and different ideas. For example, if the problem you are working on is how to best transport product between buildings ask the group to give you examples of how things are transported in these different areas:

Woodworking

Nature
Wild West

Restaurants

Publishing
Art
Medicine
Geology
Witchcraft
Politics

Comedy
War
Agriculture
Philosophy
Biology
Sports

| | |
|---|---|
| History | Chemistry |
| Metalworking | Aeronautics |
| Animals | Transportation |

Add what you want to this list. Spend enough time discussing and playing out the selected analogies so that the group has almost forgotten what they are working on. Then begin to force fit some of the more intriguing thoughts to the original problem.

**Braintickler #23 - Irrelevant objects**

Here we use irrelevant objects to create analogies and connections to stimulate the generation of new ideas. I used to keep a large container of objects, some of which were quite strange and put them on a table. I figured it was better to have a real object to display. Of course the disadvantage is that you are limited in size. When the time came to trigger some new ideas I would have people select a few of these objects and identify connections they may have to the problem at hand. But you may want to develop a list of irrelevant objects by passing out catalogues or magazines and having people shout out some of the ones that seem strange and disconnected or by just having folks brainstorm a list.

The next step is to pick some of these objects and discuss their characteristics and why they are good analogies to the problem at hand. Then capture some new ideas based on this discussion.

**Braintickler #24 - Idea Gardens**

I've had a passion for gardening pretty much most of my life. Gardening can be a rich metaphor for the stimulating of thoughts about creating organizational breakthrough.

In a garden we:

94

- Plan
- Plant things (seeds, seedlings, and established plants)
- Re-arrange
- Fertilize
- Weed
- Remove bugs
- Prune
- Till soil
- Pinch back flowers
- Let wildflowers grow
- Pick flowers
- Add statuary
- Create walkways
- Protect from elements

Each one of these activities has a parallel with some breakthrough activity in an organization. For example, how might we seed and fertilize the ideas within our organization? What part might pruning play in the stimulation of breakthrough ideas? What are things we might consider pests that influence new thinking and what can we do to combat them? How might we till the soil to help the creative/innovative process?

As you can see, the use of this metaphor allows us to pose some challenging questions while letting us carry out the conversations in a context well outside the normal thinking process.

**Braintickler #25 - Visual metaphors**

With this technique a series of pictures are used as metaphors to expand the thinking process. The starting point is to put together a series of interesting pictures not necessarily related to the problem on which you are working. I once had a large collection of these on Kodak slides which I would flash on a slide projector (anyone remember these?). These days you can gather a great selection just by roaming around on the internet.

The object is to have people individually write down things that come to mind as they view these pictures. Show ten or more pictures and then ask them to identify connections or interesting thoughts related to the problem. Then go on to brainstorming possible solutions or ideas based on these observations.

## Brainwriting

I think of these as a separate group because they are primarily non-verbal techniques. Whether you are passing index cards with ideas around the table or flying paper airplanes with ideas on them around the room (which is a blast), it's done without talking. This removes any inhibitions people may have to talk or the tendency of some to talk too much or get off track. It also gets everyone involved.

There are lots of ways to carry out brainwriting sessions. A simple way is to begin with a problem statement and then have participants jot down their ideas on index cards or sticky notes. They may then either place them on the table or pass them to the person next to them. When someone temporarily runs out of ideas they pick up another index card or sticky note and use the ideas contained on these to develop new thoughts. Various alternatives include posting sticky notes on the wall, sending ideas around the room on paper airplanes, or anything else you can come up with. Make it a fun process. During one session I had people write their ideas on sticky notes and stick them on various parts of their bodies. We had a great time with this one and it was very, very productive.

After a brainwriting session there needs to be a process to evaluate ideas. The group that participates in the process of creating the ideas should have a chance at the end to be a part of this process.

Well there are a few ideas for some of the more rational techniques of brainstorming. There are more to come! In the next chapter we'll take a look at a number of ways to get your group into a highly creative frame of mind.

# Chapter 4

# Group Mental Gymnastics
and Warm-ups

The purpose of this chapter is to take a look at some great techniques for getting you and your group into a very creative zone. Any time that you engage in physical exercise it's a good idea to stretch the muscles. So why not stretch the mental muscles prior to engaging in mental exercises? Groups that just plunge into the ideation process often start from a *stuck* state. These techniques will help to get them out of their *stuckness*. Feel free to put your own *Kentucky Windage* on these techniques. And let each of them trigger new possibilities. I'd love your feedback on these and also your thoughts on techniques that have worked for you. What are your favorite techniques? What has worked particularly well for you? Let me know.

## Warm-Ups and Diversions

Use these whenever you need to pump a group, or yourself, up. This may be at the beginning of an ideation session or just when you really want a group to stretch its thinking. It is often useful to do these exercises when a group is at a low point in its idea output. A correctly chosen diversion can do a lot to get them re-focused and re-energized.

## 1. Let's go exploring

Following is a list of interesting thoughts. Feel free to add some of your own. Distribute these to individuals, pairs, or triads in your group and ask them to spend a few minutes discussing the significance of these thoughts to the situation at hand. You may want to give two to each group or individual so they have a choice in case one doesn't move them. Fun and laughter are highly encouraged as usual and anything goes. During the sharing process let others contribute as you see fit.

- Indecision is the key to flexibility.
- You can't tell which way the train went by looking at the tracks.
- There is absolutely no substitute for genuine lack of preparation.
- Nostalgia isn't what it used to be.
- Sometimes too much to drink isn't enough.
- The facts, although they may be interesting, are irrelevant.
- Someone who thinks logically provides a nice contrast to the real world.
- Things are more like they are today than they ever were before.
- Everything should be made as simple as possible, but no simpler.
- Friends may come and go, but enemies accumulate.
- I have seen the truth and it makes no sense.
- This is probably as bad as it gets, but don't count on it.
- If you think there is good in everyone, then you haven't met everyone.
- All other things being equal, fat people use more soap.
- If you can smile when things go wrong, you have someone else in mind to blame.
- One seventh of your life is spent on Mondays.
- By the time you make ends meet, the ends move.
- Not one shred of evidence supports the notion that life is serious.
- The more you run over a dead cat, the flatter it gets.
- There's more than one way to skin a cat, but you always end up with cat skin.

## 2. Whine and jeez parties

Whining is one of the most interesting outlets you'll ever find. After five or ten minutes of loud, unabashed, serious whining you'll feel better and have an open channel for some new thinking. This technique gives people permission to do something they've probably wanted to do for a long time but couldn't. Here's a chance to get it all out. Just have the whole group walk around and whine about anything that comes to mind. It could be real problems they face or silly things they make up. It really doesn't matter. What matters is that it is done with complete freedom and the exercise is perceived as a lot of fun.

When it's over have people talk about the experience. How do they feel right now? What new thoughts have taken up the space previously occupied by those things that were able to whine about? Then move on into another ideation technique using the whined-out minds.

If you need a jump-start on things to whine about you'll find them in Appendix H. Or call me for some lessons. We'll spend a little time on the phone whining. Just call me at Dial-A-Whine 352-552-5973 and remember, *whining* is just a few letters away from *winning*.

## 3. Silly words

Often some of the most creative thinking within groups comes when trying to attach meaning to a meaningless word. Try this task out in small groups and see if it doesn't raise some really different thinking and create a lot of laughter in the process. Each group gets a word of their own to work on and needs about 5 minutes to answer the following questions which they will then share with the total group. To add some more *oomph* to the process have people add to this word list.

What does this word mean? How would you know if you saw one or if it happened to you? In what ways might it benefit you and your organization?

Fratigumptuous

Paridigamial

Valumanian

Skreeter

Thinkamut

Transqualimation

Microsoftie

Forceptitute

## 4. Stupid questions

In the mid-eighties *The Book of Questions* by Gregory Stock was a popular mini-book which contained a number of rather serious questions designed to create group dialogue. A follow up spoof called the *Book of Stupid Questions* by Tom Weller came out shortly after and I took a few of these questions and used them to warm-up a group's thinking for a session we were doing. The results were great and I've used them often with groups. Here are a few sample questions from various sources to get you started. You may elect to have them just develop their own *stupid questions* in small groups. Of course, one of the overriding lessons here is that there really are no *stupid questions*.

- If you crossed the International Date Line on your birthday would you still get presents?

- If you found you had been mix up in the hospital as a baby, would you turn yourself in?

- Have you ever had an out of body experience? How do you know?

- What kind of hen lays extra large eggs?

- If nothing sticks to Teflon, how do they get Teflon to stick to the pan?

- If you play your portable radio louder do the batteries wear out more quickly?

- Where does lint come from?

- Would you rather be extremely happy but not know it or be miserable and not care?

- What is your favorite toe? Why?

- Would you like to be a member of the opposite sex? Why? How do you know you're not?

- If you could change the order of the alphabet, what order would you put the numbers in?

- What is your favorite internal organ?

- When a fly alights on a ceiling does it do a loop or a roll to get into position?

- What happens to donut holes when you eat the donut?

There are a number of ways to use these questions in group sessions. I've found it to be quite successful when groups of three are given a question and a few minutes to collaborate on their answers followed by general group sharing. Another possibility might be to post them in the meeting area and have people add their remarks during breaks.

## 5. Totally useless skills

I first had the pleasure of seeing Rick Davis when he did a presentation at a Humor Conference in Saratoga, New York. Rick has a group called *The Institute for Totally Useless Skills* at 20 Richmond Street in Dover, New Hampshire, 03820. I have often used some of the skills I learned from Rick as diversions in my own workshops. These *include disappearing body parts, arm stretching, two noses, yodeling, spoon hanging* and many others. Sound intriguing? These activities are a great deal of fun and, more importantly, can really get people to free up some new thinking. Contact Rick for his book (Totally Useless Office Skills) and/or video. Or visit his website by searching on the book title.

## 6. Image streaming

This technique involves a *no-holds-barred* dumping of images about whatever topic people are working on. The idea is to download any images, thoughts, feelings, and pre or misconceptions about the problem or opportunity being addressed. Everyone comes loaded with pre-conceived notions regarding most any topic and these can create blockages in thinking that can greatly reduce creative capacity. The process question to get a group started in image streaming is simply:

What thoughts come into you mind when you think of _____?

Track these images in as few words as possible and post them so that people can refer to them as fodder in the creative process.

## 7. Job titles

I'm convinced that, for many of us, our current job titles determine how we think. If your title is *director* or *manager*, you tend to think like one (whatever that means). If your business card says you're an *administrative assistant*, then that's probably the way you'll think and act. In a number of workshops I've asked people to invent a new job title which describes what they would really like to be – or do. When I started my business a few years ago I decided to give my self the title of *president*. It sounded impressive. After a while I decided that it wasn't all that exciting and it certainly didn't describe what I wanted to be doing. Let's face it; the president of a one-person firm is not exactly something to write home about. I actually have a friend (let's call him Joe) who has a company called Joe, Inc. and a title of president and CEO.

So I changed my title to *Raging, Inexorable, Thunder-Lizard Creativity Evangelist* and later to *Wicked Good Slayer of Organizational Sacred Cows* (I toyed with the idea of carrying a sword but decided against it since the airlines frowned upon it). I've recently changed it to *Cerebral Proctologist*. I think I lost a few customers with that one. Nothing says we have to keep titles for that long so I change mine when I find something that better describes what I do.

This warm-up exercise asks participants to scratch out the present title on their business card and change it to something that excites them. In Appendix G you'll find my collection of job titles. Feel free to use this to stimulate new ideas or simply borrow a title if it appeals to you. This is one of those exercises that have the capability of a lasting impact on people. An exciting and different title sets people apart from the normal and elevates their feelings of self worth a great deal.

## 8. Question storming

Question storming is similar to image streaming except that it focuses in on brainstorming all the questions that come to mind about a problem or opportunity. I find it useful to get people to stretch their thinking about questions by asking them to identify at least three really stupid questions. The idea is to make it
OK to ask these questions because most people are a little hesitant to ask them. Just telling people that there are no stupid questions doesn't always work. You need to let them practice how to identify and accept them, and how to use them as a means of really stretching the thinking.

## 9. Opera singing

And now for something completely different! When a group is really in a rut regarding how it conducts its meetings it's time to really liven things up and change the rules completely. Why not conduct your meeting as a light opera. Rather than speaking, people must sing to each other (and perhaps even throw in some show biz animation). Who knows - you may get to like it and want to conduct all your meetings that way!

The idea is to do something different that really disrupts existing patterns - and is fun. Other alternatives might include:

- Stand-up meetings
- Blind-folded meetings
- Person talking stand on one leg
- Talk in different (or contrived) language
- Totally non-verbal meetings
- Sculpturing, acting, or drawing out thoughts
- Using sign language
- Whispering, or yelling

## 10. What do you call this?

This technique is useful when you want a quick and easy way to disrupt thinking patterns. Simply have everyone walk around identifying particular objects and giving them new names. For example, look at the overhead projector and say, "What a nice car". Then move on to the lamp hanging from the wall and say, "Nice doggy". The whole thing sounds a little foolish, doesn't it? It is. And that's why it works. Sometimes you really need to get pretty silly to create thinking shifts. Have fun with this one.

## 11. What does rock n' roll smell like?

I first saw this technique use by one of my early mentors, Sidney Shore. It involves getting connected to various objects through senses not normally used. For example, we use vision and smell usually to sense roses. But what does a great rose sound like? A great old Dizzy Gilespie recording sounds wonderful. But what does it feel or smell like?

Take a few minutes and try to:

> See what you can hear.
> Hear what you can touch.
> Feel what you can smell.
> Smell what you can see.

Listen to the smell of a delightful perfume. What might you hear? See the sound of some instruments in an orchestra. What does the sound of a flute look like to you? What does the sound of the bass drum look like? How does red feel to you? How does the blue sky feel to your touch? How does gray flannel taste to you?

Now use this to create some new thoughts around your problem or opportunity. What possibilities arise from looking at it using all the different senses? What does that highly visible product you are working on smell like, sound like, feel like? What is the smell of a creative solution to your problem? If your problem was a musical piece, what would it sound like?

## 12. Silly photos

We occasionally need to be reminded that life is just not that serious. One way of doing this is to create picture galleries showing group or team members at their absolute silliest. You can use portrait booths, smart phones, or digital cameras. With digital pictures you can use a number of programs to make the results even sillier. Going digital here also will make it easy to create a silly gallery since you can easily create an album and print out color copies for everyone. Smart phones and tablets make it easy to create these pictures

When things get a little too serious and the creative thinking is getting a bit pinched, just asked them to take a quick look at themselves in the gallery. Talk about quick changes!

## 13. Ask the kid

Sometimes what you are really after is to bring out the kid in each of your team members. One way I've found useful is to give people the opportunity to explain the problem or opportunity to a kindergartner. You may want to create a real opportunity for this to happen or have people pair up, one being an incredibly intelligent, but jaded, professional and the other being a bone-headed, open-minded kid. The person playing the grown-up tries to bring it down to the kindergartner's intelligence level (which might not be much of a stretch for some of us) and the kindergartner tries to ask as many dumb questions as possible (remembering, of course, that there are really no dumb questions). Great fun - and a great learning experience as well.

In some of my past workshops I've asked people to bring in pictures of themselves as children. We then create a gallery of these pictures and possibly even a contest of some sort to name these kids. But the important part of this exercise is that everyone will be able to ask his or her own kid self for advice anytime they want to. Imagine being able to overcome some of your thinking constraints by confronting your self as a child. Wild! Give it a try.

## 14. Human cameras

Ever wonder what it's like to be a camera? The only time you have vision is when someone decides to open your shutter and let you in on a split second shot of what's in front of you. Think of how different that is from our normal constant visual connection with the world around us. Here's a chance to be a camera and let your newfound experience give you a new perspective on everything around you. This may be particularly effective in a setting where there are a number of visuals that are meaningful to the problem or opportunity being worked on.

Done in pairs where one person is the photographer and the other is the camera. The photographer leads the camera around until s/he wants to take a picture. The camera's eyes are closed until the photographer snaps the picture by squeezing the right shoulder. The eyes open for about a second and record what they see. Take several pictures this way and then unload and develop the film. What did you see? What didn't you see? What specific thoughts relative to your current work came from the experience? Switch partners half way through so each one can experience being a camera. With this technique it is good to follow the pairs experience with a larger group discussion.

## 15. Grateful Dead stereo caskets

Talk about a strange warm-up! One fine day it occurred to me that people spend a small fortune on caskets to bury their loved ones. The person being buried has no time to enjoy this fine casket while s/he's alive. Wouldn't it be nice if we could find ways to use caskets while we're living? So we created a mock company to produce life-enhancing caskets.

Our first product is the *Grateful Dead Stereo Coffin*. The point of this exercise is to come up with as many possibilities as you can to utilize a coffin for enjoyment in this lifetime. Don't be afraid to have a lot of fun with this one. In past groups we've developed several hundred possibilities and, if this book doesn't make it, I may just start a business here.

The object of this task is to develop as many other products as you can in a short time period. Have people start with about 5 minutes of individual thought about how to use their casket while they're living and then begin a brainstorming session. Use this to warm people up and to introduce them to the brainstorming process and guidelines.

## 16. Captionless cartoons

The idea here is to provide groups with cartoon that have had their captions removed. The object is to have them generate new captions. If tried this several times as a diversionary break and it work very well. It doesn't create a whole lot of new thought but it sure does a good job of getting minds away from the work for a while. And it always provides some great laughs that will re-kindle the creative juices.

## 17. Quotations exercise

This is one of my favorite ways to warm-up a group. I usually have quotations on index cards and give each person a couple to look at. It can also be done in pairs or small groups depending on your needs. The object is to provide people with some quotations that really stimulate their thoughts relative to the task at hand and to begin helping them to challenge the rules. The process questions might be:

112

♦ What are the implications of this quotation to our project or task?

♦ Based on this, how might I/we challenge our current thinking patterns regarding our work?

♦ How might the contents of this quotation raise our level of thinking in the work we are about to do and create more opportunity?

You'll find a short collection of quotations to get you started in Appendix B. If you want a spectacular collection then get your hands on my Kindle book, ***Quotations to Tickle Your Brain***. This is my collection of some of the best quotations that focus on creative thinking.

## 18. The Elizabethan insult kit

Sometimes it helps to release your inner aggression so that your creative thoughts will have an easier time making their way to the surface. One way to do this is to spend some time in a rather hilarious process of insulting everyone in the group. I do this with the help of a kit from Jerry Maguire, an English teacher from Greenwood, Indiana. The purpose is to just let everyone loose for a certain amount of time so that they can insult as many of their associates as they can. This is done by merely picking at random one word from each column and using these to insult everyone you come in contact with. Be careful not to spit as you become more aggressive in this exercise – you *droning, beetle-headed, hedge-pig*.

**Elizabethan Insult Kit**

| Column 1 | Column 2 | Column 3 |
| --- | --- | --- |
| bawdy | bat-fowling | baggage |
| beslobering | beef-witted | barnacle |
| churlish | beetle-headed | boar-pig |
| craven | clay-brained | canker-blossom |
| curlish | crook-pated | clotpole |
| droning | dizzy-eyed | dogheart |
| fawning | earth-vexing | dewberry |
| fobbing | elf-skinned | flap-dragon |
| frothy | fat-kidneyed | foot-licker |
| goatish | fly-bitten | fustilarian |
| impertient | fool-born | giglet |
| jarring | gut-gripping | harpy |
| Logger-headed | halk-faced | hedge-pig |
| lumpish | hasty-witted | horn-beast |
| mammering | hedge-born | jolthead |
| mewling | idle-headed | lout |

Try some creative ways of using this. Use it in people introductions or greet people at the door by insulting them.

## 19. Ugly faces

The behavior of many people in meetings is dominated by the need to look good. Therefore, there is a strong tendency to not take risks because it may make you look bad. So I start many of my sessions by helping people to practice looking bad. Just having them turn to the person on either side of them and make an ugly face is all that may be necessary. Repeat every now and then as necessary because people may tend to return to their need to look good.

You may want to have people get up and walk around so that they can make ugly faces at more of their associates. Try taking instant or digital pictures of people at their worst and hanging the results up in the gallery. Give an award to the ugliest face. Why stick with the face? Challenge people to make monsters out of themselves and have a 5-minute monster walk. Have ugliest outfit day at the office or *Halloween in July* day. Pass out spinach at your meeting and have everyone dangle a large piece of spinach from his or her front teeth. Things may never be the same again.

## 20. The big flush

People bring lots of things with them to meetings that get in the way - hidden agendas, outdated rules, self-limiting thoughts etc. Thinking can be moved up several notches if these limiting thoughts can be purged. At one meeting in an organization that seemed to be ruled by old patterns of thinking, I decided to try something a little different one day. I brought a roll of toilet paper with me and handed out generous amounts to each person in the group.

I instructed them to think about all the rules, accepted truths, forbidden areas and sacred cows and write them each on a patch of the toilet paper. Then they were asked to read any of these they wanted to others in the group. When we all finished sharing these, we proceeded to a mass flushing in the closest restroom. I had some great feedback from that group. Apparently the acting out of

115

the flushing had a tremendous impact on getting them out of their normal thinking boxes.

You may want to try having a bonfire, bringing a small shredder to your meeting, or writing them on something edible like a candy bar and then simply eating them. Or, if you want to preserve, the statements, you could put them on *post-its* and post them on a *Thought Obituary* chart.

## 21. Silly handshakes

When working with large groups, introductions often seem to drag on forever. Sometimes introductions just aren't that important. It's more important to get things started quickly in a way that leaves people knowing each other. Here's a way to start off some meetings with a different sort of bang.

Simply instruct people to walk around and introduce themselves to everyone in the room using the silliest handshake that they can think of. And, of course, try to make each handshake a little sillier than the last one. It's good to model one for the group if you can, but then lust let them at it. You'll be quite surprised at the results. Embellish this exercise in any way you feel comfortable. I've even tried to have them use another language (or imitate one) in their introductions. You also may want to continue this in other parts of the session by having congratulatory handshakes. Or have them develop their own team's secret silly handshake

## 22. Video quips

Okay – I admit I'm a movie nut. I rarely miss a new movie and, when I do, I usually catch it in its video or streaming stage. There are very few movies from which you cannot extract a scene or two that can serve as a great stimulator for thinking. For example, in the *Dead Poet Society* there are two scenes in particular that have the potential to shift thinking. In one scene Robin Williams asks his students to all stand on his desk so that they might view the world differently. And another scene suggests they tear the introduction out of their books so it won't affect their thinking. In *Dances with Wolves*, there are some perfect examples of *dialogue* in the form of Indian tribal councils.

The use of video quips also has the advantage of providing variety in the media. Sessions using just a single media can get rather boring and a 5-minute change of pace can work wonders. By the way, audio clips may also be used which is quite a bit easier if you just don't happen to have a video setup at your disposal. Here are a few of the sources I've found for my video interludes:

The Dead Poet Society
Big
Dances with Wolves
Good Will Hunting
Karate Kid
Ghandi
The Gods Must Be Crazy
Blazing Saddles
Search for the Holy Grail
Monty Python's Flying Circus (my favorite source)
Reconstructing Harry (and most other Woody Allen films)
Candid Camera episodes
Joe and the Volcano

Add your own favorites to the list and let me know which ones you find helpful.

## 23. Stream of Consciousness

117

The idea here is to have a *no holds barred* brain dump. What has everyone come here thinking? You don't have to prime the pump. Just have people blurt out any words of thoughts they have on their mind. There are no wrong or rights – anything goes. People are allowed to build on others thoughts if they want. You may want people to verbalize their thoughts and have a facilitator quickly capture some them (or some of the key words). I recommend this be done in a way that they don't see what is being captured and that the facilitator captures these thoughts without communicating to the participants. Or you may have people write them down on post-its and hang them on charts, which is a lot easier. After these are posted have everyone look them over and have a dialogue about them. What do they mean to the problem at hand? What possibilities do they suggest? Another benefit of this warm-up is that it gets things off people's minds to prepare them for ideating. Also, the results may be useful later as triggers in the ideation session.

## 24. You are what you say - and how you say it

There are a number of studies that suggest that the words you use and the accompanying non-verbals play a strong part in determining the results of your actions. We probably don't need studies to tell us this. When you use happy, pleasant words and act in happy, pleasant ways the results of your behavior will likely be positive. And the same logic goes for the use of unhappy, negative words and actions. Happy words recall positive things from your past and unhappy words recall negative ones. What this means is that you can have a powerful impact on results by using the right words and non-verbals. And you don't even have to be in the right frame of mind to do it. Even a group that is in a very negative frame of mind can raise the positive level of their action by forcing themselves to use the right words.

I've often illustrated this in my presentations and workshops by asking people to conduct two one minute conversations using each of the following lists of words. The task is to carry out a conversation with another person for one minute using as many of the words and associated non-verbals, starting with the *unhappy* list first. Try it sometime. You'll be quite amazed at the results.

| Unhappy, negative words | Happy, positive words |
|---|---|
| Unhappy | Joyful |
| Upset | Mirthful |
| Tears | Joking |
| Depressed | Giggle |
| Sullen | Happy |
| Dark | Laughter |
| Morose | Glad |
| Sad | Jolly |
| Dismal | Silly |
| Hopeless | Cheerful |
| Bleak | Amusement |
| Sorrow | Merriment |
| Misery | Delightful |
| Negative | Fun |
| Somber | Jovial |

## 25. Factoids

From time to time people involved in group creative activities need to take some time out and stretch their minds. It's just like physical stretching exercises during training. One way of doing this is to use what I call factoids. These are short, interesting, surprising facts that can stimulate dialogue regarding the problem or opportunity at hand. Use them in any way you find suitable for your situation. I have used them as table topics by putting them on index cards at tables (or under chairs) and asking people to share a few of these and discuss the possible connection to what they are doing. It's great if you can connect them to the problems or opportunities that the group is addressing. What thoughts does this factoid trigger about or work? In what way does it help you to stretch your thinking about the problem or opportunity?

Appendix J has enough facts to keep you busy for a good long time. Select a few intriguing ones from there to get you started.

## 26. Humor breaks

All meetings can get tense after a certain time. Taking a humor break can be a simple and effective way to release tensions and get people back into the proper frames of mind for some creative thinking. YouTube is a goldmine of great comedy sketches (Tim Conway's dentist sketch is my all-time favorite). Oldies like Candid Camera, Monty Python, or Mr. Bean are always great. You need to be sensitive to the use of un-censored material lest you offend someone in the group. Other possibilities may be to use jokes or cartoons. I've probably said this before, but humor is one of the greatest lubricants I know of for releasing the creativity in people. When all else fails – lighten up!

## 27. Symbols, mottos, logos, and songs

I've found this technique to be particularly useful with project teams. The idea is to have the team develop something that will serve as a lasting anchor to add excitement to their effort. It doesn't hurt to turn this one into a lot of fun as well. If the team is large enough you may want to divide up the work. One group works on a song, one on a motto, one on a logo, and one on a symbol. Have them act these out as necessary and don't forget to include the opportunity of having each group provide a little added input to each other's output. The output should be made as graphical as possible so that it can be posted later (and perhaps added to) in the team area.

## 28. Become your problem

One of the most powerful ways to warm up groups working on a common problem or opportunity is to have them *become* what they're working on. This is very useful when the work involves a product or a system. I recall a group I was working with recently whose job was to develop future product portfolios for HVAC (heating, ventilating, and air conditioning) systems for cars. Rather than having them work from their existing mindsets I decided to have them become various components of the system. One group became the controls, one became the ducts, and one became the heat exchangers, and so on. Their task was to ask how it felt to be that system, what they liked and disliked about it, how they felt about their neighbors, what their goals where, what turned them on and off, and any other general observations. An advanced group may even want to try acting out their new role. The idea is to really get them into playing the part of something so that they may really understand it from an internal perspective. Make sure to track some key thoughts from this activity because they are likely to be quite useful areas to build on later in the ideation process.

## 29. Oxymorons and redundancies

For those who have never heard this word, oxymorons are two (or more) words that are sometimes seen together – but don't quite fit. Here are a few oxymoron examples:

| | |
|---|---|
| Senate ethics | military intelligence |
| professional wrestling | highly depressed |
| Army intelligence | true replica |
| plastic glass | tremendously small |
| elevated subway | airline food |
| live recording | slightly pregnant |
| working vacation | chaotic organization |
| even odds | legal brief |

And a few examples of redundancies:

| | |
|---|---|
| Jewish synagogue | basic fundamentals |
| new initiative | lag behind |
| general public | plan ahead |
| future plans | join together |
| personal friend | gather together |

What are some *oxymorons* and redundancies that relate to the group's problem and what do they suggest?

## 30. Organizational Heimlick maneuvers

Heimlick maneuvers are designed to dislodge items that are causing people, or in this case, organizations, to choke. Many organizations are choking on their own rules and traditions. The object here is to develop list of things that are currently choking out the ability to create breakthrough. Acting out the maneuver in some way adds more realism and fun to the process. Here's one way to do it.

Instruct everyone to write down rules, traditions, and paradigms that are controlling and blocking their thinking on small pieces of paper. Roll these into small balls and pair up with another person. Put a few in your mouth and have the other person act out a Hiemlich maneuver on you while spit out the balls of paper. Then reverse positions. Sound crazy? It is! But getting a little crazy is what you need to do if you really want to create some thinking shifts.

## 31. Airbags, cow chips and panty hose

It is sometimes a good idea to have a warm-up session prior to a brainstorming session and one option is to use some rather strange objects and generate as many new uses for them as you can in the group. You can use common items like brick or paper clips if you want. But wouldn't it be more interesting to think of new uses for cow chips, panty hose, old tires, road kill, or air bags? I am personally working on new air bag products and would be interested in any ideas you might have. Currently I have airbag designs for football players, first dates, workstations (so people won't get hurt when they fall asleep and their heads hit the desk), ducks, and people that tend to walk into walls a lot.

The idea is simple. Have a group carry out a brainstorming session for uses of a common, or strange, object and identify a large amount of ideas in a short time to get the ideation mindset clicking. Here are some possibilities:

Haircut remnants
Old bottle caps
Un-matched socks
Used brake pads

LP's
Toenail clippings
Old tires
Used cat litter
Grass clippings
Used toner
Cow chips
Egg shells
Dental floss
Airbags
Used tires
Used oil
Negative feelings
Missing socks
Panty hose

## 32. Snow ball fight

I was first introduced to this by me friend Jaquie Lowell (who learned it from Ellie Katz) at a workshop in San Diego, the land of snow. The snowballs are actually bags of marshmallows and the rules are very simple. Grab as many snowballs as you can and throw them at anyone you want. It's close to impossible to get hurt with one of these no matter how hard it is thrown. The worst thing that can happen is that one gets stepped on and squished into the floor. Time the activity for about five minutes. The group will really be able to get to work after this.

## 33. Creating collages

If you can get people to do some pre-thinking about a problem or opportunity prior to a creative session it'll help them get off to a good start. Creating individual collages prior to a session is an easy and fun way to do this. Instruct everyone to collect a bunch of pictures or items that they think might have an interesting connection to what the group is working on. Have them portray them any way they want and bring them to the session. You can have them hang items around the room or make a table available. You may even want some people to explain what they brought and what connection it has to the work at hand. There will be lots of opportunities to have others add to these connections too.

This is a great way to get a group started and also creates a terrific idea stimulating area for use during the session. Again, feel free to put your own creative spin on the basic idea.

## 34. *Tweaking* the question

There are often situations where the problem or opportunity statement needs to be *tweaked*. Successively asking the "why?" question is an easy way of doing this. The answers to this question will give you added opportunities to view your problem from a different angle. Here is an example of how to test and expand a question.

In what ways can I lose weight?
  Why do I want to lose weight?
        In order to look trimmer.
In what ways can I look trimmer?
  Why do I want to look trimmer?
        To improve my self image.
In what ways might I improve my self-image?
  Why do I want to improve my self-image?
        It will help me in my business and personal life.
In what ways might I become more effective in my professional life?
  Why do I want to be more effective in my professional life?

So I may feel good about myself.
In what ways might I feel good about myself?

Continue this *tweaking* process until you are all *tweaked-out* or have all fallen to sleep.

## 35. Your assignment if you choose to accept it.

I found that giving mind-stretching tasks to small groups (5-6) is a great way to get everyone thinking differently. I'd put them on index cards and distribute them in some creative way (under every 5th chair, in random notebooks, taped on the back of every fifth person entering the room, etc.). Here are a few example tasks:

o   Think of all the sacred cows in your business and personal lives. Which are the most important for slaying and how would you do this?

o   Why is your job like a stomach? What bothers you about this and what do you like about it? What possibilities does this train of thought give you regarding your job?

o   Make up a few strange, senseless, silly words (just let them fall out) and then invent some products that would go by that name.

o   Spend the next few minutes exaggerating every item around you and calling them by wrong names. How does this make you feel? What new thinking opportunities come from this?

o Identify as many oxymorons that describe your work or personal life. What do these tell you about possible ideas for the future?

o Pick a common object in the room and identify at least 50 things you can do with it. Then identify 50 more. How might you transfer some of these to current opportunities?

o Pick a few objects that sound interesting and then become these objects in your mind. How does it feel? What new ideas does being that object bring to your mind?

o Look around you and choose five objects. Now describe these objects using as much distortion and exaggeration as you can in relaying the information about the features they naturally possess.

o Pretend you are a spy for your competition and take a fantasy trip through your organization or company taking notes of what you see. What are some potential weaknesses you see that provide you new opportunities?

o You have just read about a new discovery that the world is all contained inside a large ball that is painted blue. How does this concept change your thinking?

o Think of as many things as you can that you've never thought of before or all the things that you've never felt the need to invent.

o Interview everyone in your group about their greatest fantasies. What are some of the things they wish they had, wish they could do, or wish were true? What new ideas come to mind?

o You just landed in your spaceship on an alien planet. The people seem rather friendly and speak your language and are really interested in what you do for a living. One person in the group is an alien who has a hard time understanding what you are telling him. Explain it until he understands.

## 36. Dumb questions

This is a pretty simple but quite effective warm-up. It's based on the fact that there are no dumb questions and then goes on to pose as many *dumb* questions as possible. You need to start with a statement (or several statements) of what your objectives are. Then form groups with the task of developing the dumbest, most outrageous questions they can think of. If they are having some trouble with this then ask them to become 3 year olds, aliens, or even animals. The results of this exercise should be posted in some fashion because these questions will serve as some great fodder for more creative thoughts.

## 37. Strange introductions

Are you sick of introducing yourself or those *go around the room* introductions? Here's a chance to be really creative and to try a little viewpoint shifting in the process. The idea is to walk around and introduce yourself to everyone in the room as quickly as possible. The spin is to make yourself a fictional character. Just make one up as you go along. And you don't have to be the same character – mix it up a bit. If you'd like, you can introduced yourself as one of your favorite heroes, actors, politicians, etc. And, if you really want to add flare, try a different language – or just make one up. I guarantee that you'll surprise yourself and you'll also have a lot of fun along the way.

## 38. Organizational bumper stickers

Ah, the world of bumper stickers. They have always fascinated me. Bumper stickers are a way of making statements and putting them out for the whole world around you to see. What statements do you want to have as the bumper sticker for your group or organization? Form some small working groups and have them develop a few of these to share with the rest of the group. Develop at least one that is on the hilarious side of funny, one that is seriously obnoxious, and one that is risky. You may even come up with one that you can use in some manner to further your work. Here are a few possibilities:

- Lottery: A tax on people who are bad at math.
- Consciousness: The annoying time between naps.
- Why is "abbreviation" such a long word?
- Be nice to your kids. They'll be choosing your nursing home.
- We all live downwind.
- If the people lead then eventually the leaders will follow.
- It's lonely at the top, but you eat better.
- Sometimes I wake up Grumpy. Sometimes I let her/him sleep.
- Change is inevitable, except in vending machines.

- Your kid may be an honor student but you're still an idiot.
- Why be normal?
- Subvert the dominant paradigm.
- Minds are like parachutes, they only function when open.
- My karma ran over your dogma.
- Everything I know is a result of my ignorance.
- Compost happens.
- Guns cause crimes like flies cause garbage.
- Rugby – elegant violence.
- They are not hot flashes – they are power surges.
- Enjoy life- this is not a dress rehearsal.
- A bad day fishing is still better than a good day at work.
- Alcohol and calculus don't mix. Never drink and derive.
- In dog years, I'm dead.
- Gravity – It's not just a good idea. It's the law.
- If at first you don't succeed, skydiving isn't for you.
- Get a new car for your spouse. It'll be a great trade.
- Old age comes at a bad time.
- The more you complain the longer God makes you live.
- Earth first! We'll strip-mine the other planets later.
- If you can read this I can hit my brakes and sue you.
- Sure you can trust the government. Just ask an Indian.
- If we are what we eat, I'm cheap, fast, and easy.
- Stop repeat offenders. Don't re-elect them.
- Fake it until you make it.
- Minds are like parachutes. They only function when open.

- Just undo it.
- We have enough youth. How about a fountain of smart?
- Question authority.
- Politicians and diapers need to be changed often for the same reason.
- Enjoy life. This is not a dress rehearsal.
- Forget world peace. Visualize using your turn signal.
- Stupidity should be painful.
- New York – where politicians make our license plates.

## 39. Silly walks

This is one of my all-time favorites. It's one of those activities that people remember for a long time and it stays in their minds as a strong anchor for bringing out the creativity. The idea is to create a *walk* of the innovative organization. The best model to kick this activity off is the famous *Ministry of Silly Walks* routine from the *Monty Python Flying Circus*. This hilarious sketch (I've seen it over a hundred times and still laugh) has the power to get people to really take risks in developing their own *silly walks*. It's readily available on YouTube.

Form groups of 4 or 5 and give them about 10 minutes to develop a walk that portrays the way they would walk if they ever reached the pinnacle of creativity and innovation. I have also had groups develop the walk of today's organization just so they can illustrate the contrast between today and the desired future. Spice this one up with a prize for the silliest walk if you'd like. And make sure everyone walks into the office the next day using their new walk.

## 40. The imagination list

If you are about to begin a session where having a vivid imagination is important then here are a few questions to help warm-up their ability to create different images.

1. What color is the letter "T"?
2. What does happiness look like?
3. What color is today?
4. What does purple taste like?
5. What does your self-image sound like?
6. What texture is the color green?
7. What does love look like?
8. What is your favorite sense?
9. What color is your favorite song?
10. What texture is your favorite scent?
11. What does winter look like?
12. What sex is the number 6?
13. How old is the letter "P"?
14. How does the letter 'M" feel?
15. What color is the fragrance of soap?
16. What does a cloud sound like?
17. What is the weight of anger?
18. What is the shape of your imagination?
19. What does your favorite book feel like?

## 41. *Just Imagine* Drive

While stuffing a bunch of books in an envelope for shipping I happen to notice the address of the envelope maker. They were located on *Just Imagine Drive* in a town in Illinois. What a great name for a street! Then I began thinking about the possibility of having people stretch their thinking by developing names of streets they would like to live on. Try it someday if you get a chance. Have people identify a few names of streets they would love to live on and then use these names as triggers during part of their workshop. The street names would most likely actually be metaphors for what they really want to get out of their life and their work.

## 42. How can we get ourselves fired?

This is probably not an exercise you want to do in an organization where there is talk of downsizing. The point of this is to bring out some real crazy thinking by brainstorming the question:

In what ways might we get ourselves fired?

This should be a no holds barred, take it to the limits, ideation process. Coming up with as many outrageous ways to get you all fired is bound to produce some great triggers for new ideas to create new breakthrough for the future.

## 43. Year 3000

In their book, *Brainticklers*, Rod Beckstrom and Elizabeth Arnold ask questions that help us ponder what life will be like in the year 3000. They feel that this frees the creativity. If you want people to think about things five years out, ask them to look out ten. If you want them to look 10 years out ask them to look 100 years out. That extra stretch gives people the creative freedom and it's a great way to warm up the thinking.

## 44. The Martians are Coming

What if Martians attacked you? What things about how you carry out your business would seem strange to them? What questions might they ask you? What things would frighten them or confuse them about you? What are the things that would most interest them and the things that they would care less about? Act it out. Have a few people in your group play the Martians and have others role-play various activities or jobs in your organization. You may also use other pretend clueless groups such as monkeys, rock bands, or CEO's.

Well, if these can't warm your group up, nothing can. Many of these techniques may seem a bit risky but go for it anyway. If you really want to bump thinking up to a higher level you need to try some things that may seem uncomfortable at first. Good luck – and have fun.

# Chapter 5

## A Few More Rather Off the Wall Braintickling Techniques

Following are a few more off the wall techniques for stimulating creative thinking. Remember to feel free to put your own spin on these so they fit your own particular situation. Most of all have as much fun as you possibly can with them and they'll reward you with some wonderful new possibilities.

## 1. **Think tank**

Find yourself a small fish tank and fill it full of idea triggers. You can make up your own or use the list below. Pass it around and have people extract these triggers from the tank and generate new ideas based on them. Each person could take the trigger and generate their own ideas or you could generate new group ideas together as new triggers are drawn from the tank.

Of course you don't really need a tank - but it makes it more fun. Some alternatives include:
- Putting the thoughts into a toy truck and driving it around from person to person.
- Writing the ideas on index cards and passing them around.
- Taping them under chairs.
- Hiding them in various locations around the meeting area.
- Taping them on people's backs.
- Locate charts in various parts of the room with idea tickling suggestions.

Here are a few triggers to get you started:

What is the opposite of the problem?
Pick a few new technologies and use them.
What if you were in the last century and had this problem?
Fantasize. Ask "What if?"

If your problem were a flower what would it be? Why?

Give a name to your problem.

How would Einstein solve this problem?

What suggestion would really make me look stupid?

What are some rules about this that can't be broken and how might I break them?

What would my favorite hero suggest about this?

If this problem were an animal what would it be?

What, in nature, comes to mind when I think about this?

If this problem disappeared what other problem would take its place?

What color describes this problem?

If I could give this problem a boy or girl name, what would it be? Why?

What is good about this problem?

What are my assumptions about this and what can I change regarding these assumptions?

## 2. *Re-ing*

Under the prefix RE- in the dictionary you'll find a long list of ways to change and challenge your thinking. Pick a dozen or so of these words and apply them to your own problem or opportunity.

For example:

| | | |
|---|---|---|
| reaffirm | reconfirm | reelect |
| recycle | reconnect | reformulate |
| reappear | recreate | reframe |
| reassemble | recopy | remarry |
| reappraise | rededicate | reintrench |
| reattach | redemonstrate | remix |
| reawaken | redesign | reprocess |
| recheck | redistribute | realign |
| recolonize | reject | |

I guess I saved you the task of finding a dictionary. You should have no problem stimulating some interesting ideas with this list.

## 3. Successive stages of impossible

To really get into the creative zone it's necessary to stretch well outside the comfort zone. One way is to ask successively more challenging questions regarding the problem or opportunity.

- What's impossible to do now?
- What's really impossible to do?
- What is impossible and totally ridiculous to think of?
- What are some things that are so utterly insane that, just by thinking about them, would get you fired, or locked up?

Remember that you can always come back from totally outrageous to a very creative idea. It's not always as easy working your way forward to that same idea.

## 4. Tabloid news

Here's a way to get a group into some really strange thought areas. And I'm going to let you do the work. It involves using headlines from tabloid newspapers (a recent article about Hilary Clinton having an alien baby comes to mind) to trigger new thinking. The stranger the headline, the better. Have your group collect article headlines and then share with the rest of the group. Follow this by having them identify ideas that are triggered by these headlines. Don't let this turn you into a tabloid junkie.

## 5. The *Be, Go, Think, Do* Model

This is a combination of several techniques that I've used as a very useful thinking tool. It pretty much summarizes your options for thinking out of the box – and is also very easy to remember. These don't have to be done in any particular order. The first option is the *Be* option. Become someone, or something, else and look at the problem or opportunity from that perspective. Trade business cards with others and become them. Become your competition, your stockholders, your customer, or just your favorite hero. Or become whatever you are working on. Remember the example of Einstein riding on the light wave? In your mind you can become, or do, anything you desire.

The next option is the *Go* option. This is where you take an excursion from your problem or opportunity and go looking for some good thinking fodder to help you trigger new ideas. Take a walk in the woods, a fantasy trip, a picture excursion, a walk in a dictionary or some catalogues, or a shopping trip in a mall. The idea is to bring back new thoughts from outside the current view of your problem.

The *Think* option refers to thinking of something else as a metaphor for your problem or opportunity. There are a number of exercises here that make use of metaphors. Refer to these or just identify a few strange ones to help you think differently. And have fun in the process! You are probably getting sick of hearing these words from me.

And finally there is the *Do* option. Just do something different to get you far enough away from your problem so the powers of mental marination can take place. Say it over a few times in your head – *Be, Go, Think, Do, Be, Go, Think, Do, Be, Go, Think, Do.*

## 6. Far out product idea stimulators

The object here is to use some interesting, and rather far-out, product ideas to trigger your own thinking as to new possibilities regarding your own problem or opportunity. Look over the varied list of products that follow, pick a few that sound intriguing, and ask how the concepts used in the design of this product might provide new thinking for your problem or opportunity.

intelligent toilets
walking desks
computer monocle screen
round refrigerators
xerographic textiles
idea salons
uphill skiing
tobacco food
spaghetti sippers
a-la-carte hotels
vegiforms
edible insects

fish dogs
computers with personality
bone phones
sonar guide canes
heating paint
peel and stick lenses
cheese whey trash bags
whining buildings
speaker paintings
wine pills
reverse mortgages
zoo doo

jack-up houses
home ATM's
smart gels
car sharing
cow's breath bug zappers
computer microwaves

hybrid cars
miniature spy planes
dog tag implants
Walkman sunglasses
photovoltaic roof shingles
car sharing

## 7. Name it and invent it

Usually we invent new products and then give them names. What if we were to reverse this process? We create a bunch of names and then proceed to invent products that live up to these names. If you have a problem to solve, perhaps you could begin by brainstorming the names of all the fictional products that would solve your problem. Then pick a few of them and use their names as triggers to further expand the thinking. Maybe an example will help to explain.

The problem you need to solve is how to create more office space for your group. Here are just a few possible names of products we could use to solve this problem:

Organizational wall stretcher
People shrinkers
Associate arks
Office silos
Fold-up furniture
Digital people

The *Organizational Wall Stretcher* sounds interesting. Let's play with this for a while.

What does a wall-stretcher suggest to you? Are there creative ways that we might use the walls to expand our office space? How about Velcro walls? Could we build more things into the walls? Could walls be movable? Could walls be removed altogether? Could walls house some balconies for stacking operations?

## 8. The Immutable Laws of Consulting

Over the years I have collected various rules, laws, and principles from various sources which I've found useful to explain behaviors in organizations and to guide my thinking in the right direction. The following are a few of these and feel free to add your own. Use these in small groups to trigger new thoughts around a problem or opportunity at hand. Or use them in larger group meetings to help people put a different spin on an opportunity. Pick a few of these that sound interesting to you and have the group brainstorm possible implications to your opportunity and suggested thinking shifts that you should explore. You may also want to put them on index cards and use them as warm-ups for a group activity. It'll start your meeting off with some laughs and some new perspectives – guaranteed. I'd really like to hear about your experiences using this technique..

*The Duncan Hines Difference:*
It tastes better when you add your own egg.

*Fisher's Fundamental Theorem:*
The better adapted you are, the less adaptable you tend to be.

*The Fourth Law of Consulting:*
If they don't hire you, don't solve their problem.

*The Fourth Law of Trust:*
    The trick of earning trust is to avoid all tricks.

*The Lone Ranger Fantasy:*
    When clients don't show their appreciation, pretend that they're stunned by your performance – but never forget that it's your fantasy, not theirs.

*Marvin's Great Secret:*
    Repeatedly curing a system that can cure itself will eventually create a system that can't.

*The Third Law of Trust:*
    People don't tell you when they stop trusting you.

*The Three-Finger Rule:*
    When you point a finger at someone, notice where the other three are pointing.

*Prescott's Pickle Principle:*
    Cucumbers get more pickled than brine gets cucumbered.

*The Law of Raspberry Jam:*
    The wider you spread it, the thinner it gets.

*The Buffalo Bridle:*
    You can make buffalo go anywhere just as long as they want to go there.

*Rhonda's First revelation:*
    It may look like a crisis, but it's only the end of an illusion.

*Romer's Rule:*
>The best way to lose something is to struggle to keep it.

*The Second Law of Consulting:*
>No matter how it looks at first, it's always a people problem.

*The White Bread Warning:*
>If you use the same recipe, you'll get the same bread.

*The Law of Common Sense*
>Never accept a drink from a urologist.

*The Law of Sacrifice*
>When you starve with a tiger, the tiger starves last.

*The Law of Avoiding Oversell*
>When putting cheese in a mousetrap, always leave room for the mouse.

*The Law of Motivation*
>Creativity is great, but plagiarism is faster.

*Law of Probable Dispersal*
>Whatever hits the fan will not be evenly distributed.

*Law of Drunkenness*
>You can't fall off the floor.

*Weinberg's Second Law*

If builders built buildings the way programmers wrote program then the first woodpecker that came along would have destroyed civilization

*Miller's Maxims*

The mind is a mismatch detector. It is easier to see what is wrong than what is right.

People do not try to disprove their own ideas.

The span of attention is limited. People seldom find anything they are not looking for. All research is done where the light is best.

## 9. The *Dark Sucker Theory*

It has always been assumed that electric light emitted light. This theory suggests that they don't emit light – they suck dark. When I read about this it reminded me of one of my all-time favorite creative triggers. I first read about it in Betty Edward's book, *Drawing on the Right Side of Your Brain*, and have used this thought often in my work.

Betty suggested that one way of bringing out your artistic talent is to try drawing the space around items rather than the items themselves. It works! When we try to draw something our capability to do so is interrupted by our knowledge about the item. For example, we know what a chair is supposed to look like and this makes it more difficult to draw it. But we have no pattern in our minds as to how the space around this chair looks. If we focus on drawing the space around the chair and try to forget that the chair is even there, guess what happens? A pretty good chair appears.

So how might you use these thoughts to come up with some creative new thinking for your problem or opportunity? If you were designing a new product, how would you think differently if you focused on the space around your product? If you normally focus on how your product interacts with the environment around it, what new possibilities come to you if you think about how the environment interacts with you product. For example, we normally think of a car driving on a road. What would change if we were to think of a road driving under the car?

There are all sorts of possibilities here for re-shaping how you think and developing new possibilities.

## 10. Describing your problem to a kindergartner

Unfortunately, most businesses don't hire 7-year olds. Think about all the fresh thinking that you could get if your staff consisted of kindergartners who didn't already know all the answers. Here's your chance to try this out and have a chance to be a kid again in the process. Separate into pairs, triad, small groups, or whatever seems appropriate. Give some people the task of explaining the problem to a group of 7-year olds and the rest of the group will become those kids. Talk like them, think like them, and ask all the stupid questions they might ask. You'll be surprised how *un-stupid* most of those questions are. You might even want to throw in a few tantrums and some whining.

## 11. Use of different senses

Last I checked, we human types had about 4 major ways to sense the world around us. We don't talk much about these; we just go about our business and use them. With this technique we go out of our way to concentrate on each of the senses. If you are working on something that you think might benefit from a multi-sense approach, give it a try. Focus separately on each of the senses (visual, auditory, touch, smell). Some think that balance and emotions are additional senses so use them if you'd like. For each one ask:

> What are some key thoughts regarding the problem that this sense brings to mind?

> What specific words describe the connection between that sense and the problem?

> How might we use this sense to enhance our opportunities or solve our problem?

Use the answers to these questions to stimulate creative ideas to solve your problem.

## 12. Defacto standards

There are certain things we assume about everything. Sometimes the name of a product spells these assumptions out for us. When we think of a clock we automatically assume that it's either digital or analog, it runs clockwise, it tells time, people use it, it has to be seen, and so on. When we think of an organization we think that it has people in it, there's a boss, it has a physical location, it has a product, and it exists to perpetuate itself. There may be a fairly long list of defecto standards for many items.

The idea here is to take a look at each one of these assumptions and then systematically refute them and come up with some creative alternatives. Sounds like fun, huh?

## 13. Creativity by moving in the wrong direction

We tend to think that improvements come from making things faster, easier to use, safer, less expensive and the like. Perhaps there are some problems, opportunities, and products that might benefit from reverse thinking. If you were designing a new car you would normally think, how might I make it faster, sportier, more economical, safer, and less expensive. What if you were to reverse the thinking in each of these areas and put your energy towards building an expensive, unsafe, un-economical, dweeby looking, dog of a car?

Sounds a little strange, doesn't it? But occasionally creative progress forward comes to us in a backward way. Forcing us to think opposite of our usual thrust will help to bring out possibilities that normally wouldn't be heard.

## 14. Nows, wows, and holy cows

This is a terrific way for an organization to take their future up a few notches (I'm beginning to sound like Emerald Lagasse). The first step is to identify some statements about the way things are today. These are the *nows* and you might create one chart for each of these since we are going to expand on them. Then, for each of these statements, identify some ways to take it up a few notches. These are the *wows*. The premise is that the best way to create a future is to identify what you can see and stand at that point and take another look. Our next look is at the holy cows. These are the statements that take each of the previous ones a step further.

With the holy cows you've created a stretch into areas far beyond where normal thinking would have taken you and some of these areas may be pretty hard to swallow. A natural development of this process might be a few scenarios along with some dialogue as to how to make them work.

## 15. You can't do that

The focus of this technique is on all the things that you can't do regarding your problem or opportunity. This is guaranteed to satisfy the pessimists in a group – and then turn them all into optimists. We tend to discount in our minds those things that we feel can't be done and then rarely come up as possibilities. So, to get around this, we start by defining the problem and brainstorming all the things that we can't do. Then the fun begins because, as you probably guessed, the next step is to generate ideas on how all those *can't's* could become *can's*. This is great for negative thinkers.

## 16.    Three ideas and a metaphor

Next time you give a group a break, require them to return with something. Give them a little extra time if you think it would help. Make it into a sort of treasure hunt. Have them bring back an object that makes an interesting metaphor regarding the current problem and 3 very weird ideas.

## 17.    Pillow ideas

Sleeping seems to have a habit of extracting great ideas from the mind. I always keep a notebook by my bedside since some of these ideas come in quickly, wake you up, and then leave just as quickly. Several years ago I took an NLP course which I found to be very intriguing. One of the techniques used was to ask your unconscious the favor each night of answering any questions you might have or helping you to solve any problems. You simply have a conversation with your unconscious, pose questions, and ask it to have the answers ready for you in the morning. I'll be honest with you – I tried it with limited results. I was able to wake up and tap into ideas that didn't seem to be there before even though the answers weren't just waiting for me. But some of my classmates had some remarkable experiences – and you might tool. It's definitely worth a try.

## 18.    Hourly Mind Explosion

The idea here is to embark at a predetermined time each hour or so and create *thought explosions* on whatever topic is being discussed. Track these thoughts throughout your session and then discuss what implications they have to your problem or opportunity.

## 19.    Going Back in Time – A Time Capsule Approach

We usually frame our thinking based on the present time. Some problems or opportunities might benefit by shifting forward or backward in time. The goal of this technique is to take you to these different time periods and, of course, to have a lot of fun in the process. If you have a large enough group you could designate a particular time frame for each group and assign them the task of becoming an ideation group within this time frame. You may even want to supply them with hats or other miscellaneous items to remind them of their time period (the Elizabethan group could

150

smear dirt on their faces, have rubber chickens, and wear appropriate hats).

Periods to focus include:

Elizabethan
Pre-historic
Revolutionary
The Sixties Generation
Star Trek/Star Wars
Shakespearean
Ozzie and Harriett and Father Knows Best

Have each group give themselves a name and then proceed to brainstorm possibilities making sure that they keep the mindsets from their own era. When they present the results they should do it using the language, and the mannerisms of that era. After each group has presented it may be a good idea to engage the whole group in a process of making new combinations based on what they've heard.

Have fun with these and make sure to give time enough for expanding the thinking on them. I've found that you need to give people some time to really play with the essence of these statements before they're ready to trigger new thinking based of them.

I think I could go on forever with techniques to stimulate creative thinking in groups but I need to leave something for my next book. I hope you have an opportunity to try some of these out and enjoy the experience! Now for a few stray thoughts on organizational breakthrough and change.

152

# Chapter 6

# Off the Beaten Path

## Miscellaneous Organizational
### *Braindroppings*

This chapter consists of some admittedly strange thought excursions. Each of these observations provides some new fodder for changing the way we think about creativity, innovation, and change in organizations. Most of these came to me while my mind was wandering (in meetings, driving my car, laying by the pool, thinking about you reading this book, gardening, etc.). They are rather spontaneous and not particularly connected. Enjoy them anyway. After reading each of the short excursions ask yourself what interesting things come to mind regarding your own situation.

## *Ozone* **Thinking for Business**

Some years ago the word *change* was hardly ever heard in organizations and now it's a part of the everyday language. It's been said, "Change is like dancing with a gorilla. You don't stop when you get tired; you stop when the gorilla gets tired." I'm beginning to think that the gorilla really likes to dance. The problem as I see it is that we tend to create change that inches us forward from our past rather than change that pulls us to a visionary future. And we tend to create surface change without getting at the thinking that goes on below the surface. When we stop pushing, everything goes back to where it was before. As consultants and trainers we can play an important role in creating breakthrough change. To do this we must be able to create some very different thinking in our client systems. I use the word, *ozone*, to suggest that it should be well outside the box.

Thinking precedes change and, if you can't influence how an organization thinks, there will never be significant change. There tends to be a pretty strong mismatch between the behaviors that stimulate creative thinking and those that are acceptable in most work environments. For example, most work environments tend to be very judgmental. When someone says or does something, everyone else feels compelled to decide whether it is right or wrong. Breakthrough thinking takes place in an environment where there are no wrong answers, everyone is supportive, and it's safe to explore areas that are new and different. There is a tendency for people in organizations these days to stay in the comfort zone and no breakthrough ever occurs from the comfort zone. Are there ways that you can help your clients explore the area outside the comfort zone?

Real creativity and breakthrough comes from going to outrageous and working back as opposed to pushing forward from the present state. It's much more powerful to go to an outrageous possible future and ask, "*Why not?*" than it is to start from today and ask, "*Why can't we?*" You'll always end up at a higher state of change and it's a lot more fun. Unfortunately, many environments don't allow outrageous thinking. It's too risky, just not professional enough, and it usually involves breaking the rules. But guess what? All breakthrough change involves breaking the rules. It's pretty hard to steal second base without leaving first. A good starting point is to ask what the rules, assumptions, and thinking patterns are regarding the business and then play with your options for breaking them. **Are there ways that you can help your clients break the rules?**

It's often difficult to overcome these thinking patterns without recognizing the value of the thinking that exists outside you own knowledge community. NIH (not invented here) is a powerful constraint in organizations and those who try to create change from within will almost always fail. There is invariably more energy within to protect the past than there is to create the future and history is loaded with examples of how outsiders were able to develop new ideas that insiders would never have been able to think of. So a part of your ozone thinking should involve bringing

155

in some outside thinkers or using techniques to help insiders really think like outsiders. **Are there ways that you can help your clients think like outsiders?**

A major component of all the behaviors that bring out creativity is the influence of humor. All indications are that most organizations take themselves much too seriously. Organizations that can loosen up and lighten up are able to produce "funtastic" results. Laughter and creativity go hand in hand but there are some other great benefits of humor. It reduces stress and induces mental and physical health. It helps create good interpersonal relationship, helps people cope with change, and stimulates improved learning. All these things have tremendous positive effects on output. If you're not using positive humor in your life and in your training you're missing out on a wonderful opportunity. Are there ways that you can use more positive humor in your life and your work?

Reduce the comfort, break the rules, think like outsiders, have fun - just a few ways to get your client into the ozone zone for some real change. Have fun and enjoy the view!

## Organizational Heimlich Maneuvers

As you may have guessed by now, I'm into the use of strange metaphors for organizational change. Organizational change can be a rough topic which people find difficult to talk about in traditional ways. A typical conversation or dialogue about change brings along with it all the patterns of thinking associated with people's feelings about their organization. And most of these have the ability to severely limit the thinking.

But, what if you were to begin a change dialogue with a question like, "How might our organization benefit from the *Hiemlich maneuver*?" First of all, it would lighten up the conversation and, in discussion of such emotionally charged issues, this is critical. A light-hearted, fun conversation is always more productive. Secondly, it allows new patterns of thinking and gives permission to people to say things they normally don't feel comfortable saying. And the content of the dialogue will have some sticking power. People will not soon forget a lively conversation on why their organization needs a *Heimlick maneuver*. The last group I did this with even created a *Hiemlick grunt* as a symbol of their need and support for change.

Use whatever metaphor you'd like for organizational change but make sure it's different enough to stimulate people and take their thinking to a completely different level. Here's a few I have used in the past:

- liposuction
- compost piles
- defibrillation
- internal body organs
- hippopotamus
- an oak tree
- panty hose

- rubber chicken
- spaghetti & meatballs
- a hard drive
- silly putty
- schools of fish
- mud slide

## The Road Through Corning

For years there have been some fairly decent highways in upstate New York, except in Corning. For some mysterious reason the highway stopped outside this city and channeled cars right through the downtown area. A few years ago a new highway opened and a friend from the area told me why it had taken so many years to do this.

The city fathers, fearing that the elimination of through traffic from the city would create an economic burden, found an old warehouse that was in way of the proposed highway. They came up with the ingenious idea of buying this warehouse and declaring it an historical landmark. This created a long battle that resulted in keeping the flow of traffic through the city for somewhere around ten years!

Now, I'm not absolutely sure this story is true but we're not too sure the *Abilene Paradox* is all that true either. But it sure reminds me of the numerous historical landmarks I've seen thrust in the way of progress in organizations. The road to organizational success is always under construction and there is never a lack of obstacles on the highway to success. Think about your own situation. What are these obstacles and what can you do about them?

## Fear of Succeeding - One Awesome Calorie

Fear of failure always comes up as the number one deterrent to creativity in the workplace. But I have seen many situations in my years in business where fear of success was responsible for drastically limiting potential accomplishments. There are many people in organizations that are trapped in situations where complete success will eliminate their jobs. And there just aren't that many people that get a rush of excitement about eliminating their own job. Many middle managers, internal consultants, and professionals who go all out to create the most effective work system they can can't help but put themselves into a position like this. I was there once myself. As a matter of fact, I probably still am as an external consultant. If I go all out to build some new and powerful creative thinking skills in my clients they won't really need me any more. I do it anyway because I've long felt that consultants should always strive to work themselves out of a job rather than building client dependency on them.

Pepsi used to have the words, *one awesome calorie*, on its cans and I'd find myself asking, "Why can't they get rid of that one silly calorie?" There may have been some scientific reason this couldn't be done. But it's also possible that the folks in the Diet Pepsi department were just concerned that, if they eliminated all the calories, there would be nothing left for them to do. I'm convinced that many of us sub-optimize our potential because of this concern about running out of things to do or reaching a pinnacle of success where the only road goes downhill. We need to leave something undone.

Are there situations in you organization or your personal life that are dictated by these feelings? If so, what can you do to assure that complete, breakthrough success will be followed by new challenges?

## Companies That Should be Innovative - But Aren't

I've been dedicated to creativity and innovation in business for many years and, for the life of me, can't understand why certain companies just seem to float along without ever coming out with anything exciting. Perhaps it's a cash cow problem. When you're busy milking your cash cows, and getting lots of milk, it's difficult to justify looking for some new and exciting drinks. But there are some companies that should be at the top of the list regarding innovative new products and services that are, in reality, at the bottom.

When was the last time you saw an exciting new product or service from Xerox, Fisher-Price, Procter & Gamble, DuPont, L.L. Bean, Corning, Hallmark, AT & T, DEC, and about 99% of the retail establishments in America? I don't mean to pick on any companies but these are just a few that come to mind. Each of them has a tremendous potential capability to be exciting. Some of them, such as Dupont, Hallmark, and P&G have invested heavily in various programs for innovation. Why is it that these programs are yielding so little in terms of bottom line innovation? I was reading recently about how DuPont has reduced its budget for books as a cost cutting measure. This may give a clue as to the answer to the previous question. How can a company claim to be interested in the thinking capability of their people and, at the same time, say they can't afford to buy them the books that they need to raise this level of thinking?

Another dynamic that seems to impact an organization's ability to create new and exciting things is their reliance on internal facilitators. Training people within organizations as facilitators is a pretty good idea. There are many situations where it is useful and effective to use internal facilitators to guide decision making. But it is rare to find a person that can do a great job of facilitating creative thinking processes from within. To bring out the best in creative thinking requires someone who can take people to where they haven't been before. Internal facilitators typically have the same mindsets of all the other people in their organizations and rarely want to risk the exploration into some possibly frightening areas.

Many facilitators, when put into a situation needing creative processes, become nothing more than voice actuated magic markers (VAMS). Their tool kits contain only a few techniques, most of which are pretty old and worn. Keeping an up to date tool kit of creative techniques is a full time job and these folks are usually too busy to do this.

There is also a tendency for organizations to select on a particular model for creative thinking and concentrate on that model. Creativity and innovation covers a lot of territory and concentrating efforts on CPS, six hat thinking, various silly instruments, or any of the other wonder drugs of creativity won't create a lasting effect for the organization.

How well does your organization tap its creative thinking capabilities?

## Creative Ubuntu

During my speaking trips to South Africa I had the pleasure of interacting with some fascinating people. In the African culture the spirit of unbuntu is often brought up as being a rather unique frame of mind in many natives. It comes from a folk saying, *Umuntu ngumunto nagabantu*, which, in Zulu, means, "A person is a person because of other people." It recognizes that you don't really exist until others recognize you. In African culture, it is an affront not to greet someone because, in essence, you are implying that they don't exist.

We don't seem to have such a word in our culture and, perhaps, we need one. If I have a great new idea does that idea really even exist until I share it, and someone else recognizes it? How many ideas literally never come into existence because they are never really recognized by others? What constitutes recognition of an idea? I have rolled these questions over in my own mind often and think it may suggest a key blockage to the creation of breakthrough thinking in organizations. You can't create breakthrough future with great ideas that never even come into existence because they aren't recognized. Ponder that one for a bit while I get into something a bit lighter.

161

# Runaway Truck Ramps and Road Memory

You're probably beginning the think that I do a lot of thinking while traveling and you're absolutely right. Flying somehow frees up my thinking - maybe it's the altitude. And where some people measure their driving in miles per hour, I measure it in ideas per mile. On a recent trip I found two very interesting highway analogies to organizational change.

Winter in the northeast creates something we call *road heaves*, especially in late winter. The roads get bumps where they never had them before. I assume that it's caused by some unhappy molecules below the surface that want to come out to check if spring has come yet. There are some roads that seem to change their shape day to day. When the weather finally warms up most of these roads go back to their original shape, leaving some *potholes* in the process. Does that mean that the road has memory? Why is your organization like one of these roads? What are the analogies between your organization and the road surface, the sub-surface, the *potholes*, and the system that allows them to all do *their thing*? Play with this for a while or try to use it in your next group dialogue.

Runaway truck ramps also intrigue me as a useful organizational tool. We seem to be in an age of programs out of control and perhaps we need the services of some organizational *runaway program ramps*. Maybe we can take advantage of the runaway ramp idea and put it to use to take away the excess energies that are causing these programs to go out of control while conserving the main vehicle. Are there some programs in your organization that are out of control? There are several organizations I know of where there is a huge reengineering truck barreling down the hill destroying everything in its way. Reengineering, done in the right way, can be very valuable. How might the runaway truck ramp analogy be used to get an out of control reengineering program back on the road?

## And Now for a Little More Bucky - The *Principle of Precession*

I discussed in an earlier chapter the idea of organizational *tensegrety* based on a word the Buckminster Fuller used to describe the balance between *tension* and *integrity*. Bucky used another term, the *principle of precession*, to explain change processes. When you spin a top, its original spinning takes place around its axis. When it slows down a secondary axis is gradually created around its original position. - the top begins to *precess* in Bucky's words. Here's your chance to go get that top that's been hanging around the house with nothing to do and give it a spin. In what ways do the dynamics of this top represent organizational change? Do the spins you put on organizational change all slow down and *precess* as things begin to sneak back to where they were? If that's the case, how might you keep the change spinning?

## Chaordic Thinking

Dee Hock is arguably one of today's most interesting management gurus. He has coined a word, *chaordic*, which represents a system which is both *chaotic* and *ordered*. This is a good word to keep in mind when thinking of creativity, innovation, and breakthrough (rather like tensegrity) because the effective thinking shifts needed in these areas must contain a lot of chaos sprinkled with a good dose of order. Dee's management principles include one on creativity which, in his own words, is as follows:

The problem is never how to get new, innovative, thoughts into your mind, but how to get the old ones out. Every mind is a room packed with archaic furniture. You must get the old furniture of what you know, think, and believe out before anything new can get in. Make an empty space in any corner of your mind, and creativity will instantly fill it.

Good advice, I'd say.

## Team vs. Individual Stardom

I once heard someone say, "Teams will flourish only when individuals have a shot at stardom." There is a critical balancing act in organizations that are team oriented involving team vs. individual creativity. Creativity is a personal thing with many individuals that they are not willing to share with other team members. When you take away their ability to be creative and to be recognized for their own personal creative abilities you may be closing down their creative thinking in team activities. On the other hand, creativity is also a group or team effort. Much of the creativity comes from people building on each other's thinking and is very synergistic.

We need to develop sensitivity to this issue and ways to make sure that a balance is achieved between individual and team creativity. We need to recognize the team effort as a vehicle for providing new sources of creative thought without ignoring the *stars* and their particular contributions. This issue becomes even more important in ideation processes that may result in patents. Who is assigned a patent in team generated ideas? What is the real origin of an idea that is the result of a dozen seeds brought together by a somewhat chaotic, creative process?

## The Perceived Unimportance of Creativity and Innovation in Business

This statement suggests the importance of creativity in the workplace:

> If I give you a dollar and you give me a dollar we both have a dollar. If I give you an idea and you give me an idea we both have two ideas.

The value of developing the creative thinking skills in your associates far exceeds that of most other development activities. And, yet, there are precious few organizations I know of that invest much of anything in advancing these thinking skills. It baffles me. I've seen the training curriculum in a number of organizations and rarely have I seen any courses that will create the skills that will take the organization to the future. Worse still, many small and medium size organizations do no training at all! The most valuable assets of any organization are its people and the most valuable thing about them is their ability to think creatively. No wonder there are so many *ho-hum* organizations in this country.

Here is another convincing piece of information regarding the importance of creativity in the future. The Nomura Institute of Japan has suggested that we are, in fact, entering an age of creativity - the agricultural age, the industrial age, the information age, and now the age of creativity where we finally begin to free up the creative resources within our organizations. Doesn't that suggest you should be interested in exploring ways to tap your creative capability?

## Proud Flesh

American Indians tell wonderful stories and have some great words and phrases that often serve as powerful metaphors for organizations. One such phrase is proud flesh. When a horse is injured its flesh heals but there is always a reminder of the injury in the feelings (or perhaps lack of feelings) around the wound. Of course, this works for humans as well.

I believe it also works in organizations. Right now there are many wounded organizations, some with rather deep flesh wounds. Some will never recover and some will recover, but never quite be able to attain the greatness they were once capable of because the proud flesh will always remind them of the wound. The only prevention for proud flesh is to assure that there are no deep wounds inflicted on the organization in the first place.

## Chinese Italian Food

We went out to eat the other night at an Italian restaurant in town that everyone raves about. This was a terrific experience but the *coup de gras* for me came when we got our doggy bags. The leftovers were given to us in Chinese food containers. Can they do that? These containers have been around since I was a kid and it's the first time I have ever seen them used by a restaurant other than Chinese. I wonder why others haven't seen this as a great alternative to the typical Styrofoam containers. I also wonder how many other good ideas like this are sitting right under our noses that we can't even see. Try to think of as many single use items as you can that may have many other potential applications. Now I'm wondering what would happen if some great Chinese and Italian cooks got together and created some really interesting combination platters.

## Miscellaneous Things I Wonder About

I may be repeating myself but I think we all need to do more wondering. Perhaps we should all set aside at least a few minutes a day for unbridled mind wandering. Let yourself wonder about anything at all - the sillier, the better. Here are a few things I wonder about.

- If they downsize at the Pentagon, could it become a triangle?
- If *con* is the opposite of *pro*, does that mean the *congress* is the opposite of *progress*?
- Are *Stay Free or Die* license plates in New Hampshire a cruel suggestion for the inmates who make them?
- When a bird flaps its wings why doesn't its body go up and down?
- Is dyslexia lexdyslia to a dyslectic?
- What is the difference between a *nook* and a *cranny*?
- Does a butterfly remember anything about its life as a caterpillar?
- Is there a job description for muckety muck?
- Do cows have conversations? "Hey, babe, come on over here and check out this really neat blade of grass!"
- If *deja vu* means you think you've experienced something before, does *vuja de* mean you think you'll experience something again?
- Why isn't *gruntled* the opposite if disgruntled?
- Does anyone really read those software agreements that are the size of Collier's encyclopedia?
- Why are compact discs wrapped the way there are? I recently bought a disc that was in the top ten. By the time I was able to get the wrapping off it had fallen to 43 on the charts.

- Why do most diarrhea ads appear on TV during the dinner hour?
- Why aren't telephone books offered on electronic media?
- If a train station is where a train stops, what is a workstation?
- If Spanish is the language of people in Spain then why isn't it called *Spainish*?

It's your turn to build a list of your own. Add at least two to the list each day and you'll eventually stumble on one that will trigger a great new idea that may change your life forever.

## The Early Death of Organizational Development

I told you these thoughts would be sporadic and disconnected!

Years ago I was one of several people to receive an early induction into a new and exciting technology that we called Organizational Development, or OD. As an Industrial Engineer and internal consultant with Kodak I personally felt this technology had a tremendous capacity to create more effective work systems. And we were able to deliver it directly to our clients because we were always in the field with them. They weren't always ready to accept the *touchy feely* stuff, but we were almost always able to create the right balance when using it because we understood, and were trusted by, our clients.

Somewhere in the growth of OD the real, practical use that focused on real change for real people in real organizations gave way to practices that were academic and often of little value in the real world. OD, which had real promise at first, became an area of practice that was actually disconnected from the constituency it was supposed to be helping. Many OD groups were, and still are, organizationally connected with human resources and contain

168

only those who have the *right* academic credentials to practice this discipline. *Right* in this case is usually defined by those in the field of OD. I feel there is such a thing as being too academic.

OD had great promise in its early stages to contribute a great deal to the effectiveness, and the creativity of organizations. This is one discipline whose practitioners have become too smart and, in the process, disconnected from their potential to have real positive impact on organizations. Come down; come down, wherever you are! We really need you.

## This Old Company

I used to watch *This Old House* a lot on public TV. It involved the rebuilding of old houses and those that have fallen into disrepair. I'm not into repairing old houses but find that the material on this program was quite nicely aligned with repairing old companies. Substitute *company* for *house* and this serves as a great metaphor for rebuilding organizations. Follow along as they rebuild and you'll notice that they nearly always have to tear down a substantial part of the substructure prior to rebuilding it. We often forget about this part as we try to rebuild our organizations for the future. If you just cover up the problems with some new facing it'll look good for a while but, sooner or later, its internal problems will create its downfall.

If you try to override the existing and faulty underpinnings of a company by overlaying new programs you may be able to create what looks like some short term gains. But the cultural underpinnings will eventually take over and have their way. For example, I've seen several situations where performance improvement programs have had seemingly positive effects. But, in the end, it just turned out to be a great cover-up to a faulty assumption about the value of people at work.

169

# Jazz as a Metaphor for Organizational Creativity

I love jazz. The more I hear it, the more I love it. It has to be the greatest American art form – period. And it's also a terrific metaphor for creativity in organizations. Years ago when I was involved in developing the *Creativity and Innovation Workshops* at Kodak I built in a module about jazz and creativity. Since then a number of books have discussed this theme (among them are Max DuPree's Leadership Jazz and John Kao's Jamming). At this point I think I could write a book about jazz and creativity but right now I just want to focus on the similarities between great jazz musicians and highly creative/innovative people in the workplace.

Great jazz musicians are able to do three things very well. They are great technicians with their instruments and are able to perform terrific solos that bring the house down. They can also perform as a perfect team player when the band is performing as a whole. The third thing they do well (and this is very important to creativity) is to provide excellent background support to others soloists. For creativity and innovation to flourish in an organization you need master technicians who are passionate and great at what they do and who can provide solos when necessary. You also need creative team players and, most importantly, creative supporting players for the other master technicians. The most creative organizations are the ones that call upon their players to perform all three functions. Team players need to show off their individual talents and receive applause every now and then or they just get lost in the team crowd. They also need time to provide strong support in helping other associates to bring out their individual talent.

I have been a jazz affectionato for as long as I can remember and have used this as a metaphor for teaching creativity for years. It was great when John Kao came out with his book, *Jamming*, which uses the analogy of jazz quite effectively to build an argument for the need for more creativity in business.

Great jazz takes full advantages of jazz musicians as individual players and as team players. Great musicians have a chance to highlight their skills in solos but, somewhere along the line, the piece always gets back into the orchestral groove. The individuals have been able to let their individual creativity shine and the band has been able to let its collective ability shine. Occasionally, a jazz piece will get chaotic and go off into space only to come back to a powerful groove, or ending. Doesn't this sound like the behavior in creative organizations?

Someday when you get a few extra minutes put on a good Miles Davis, Dave Bruebeck, or Dizzy Gillespie piece and let the music draw you a picture of the creative process in your own life and work.

## Open *Closedness*

Peter Senge coined this word that bears repeating. Many organizations claim to have so-called open door policies. This means that people are free to voice their issues and concerns with bosses. What it doesn't mean is that the bosses really care or to listen, reflect and respond. They may be open to what you have to say but may not be open to doing anything about it. It's pretty easy to listen to someone but it's not always that easy to turn that into action.

## Why Can't People Be More Like Dogs?

I've had two Golden Retrievers and sometimes think of what a great world this would be if everyone had some of their traits. I can't remember the last time my dogs got up in the morning in a bad mood or the last time they weren't happy to see me return home. I also can't remember the last time they judged anything I said or did. Everything I do is good in their eyes. Talk about unconditional love. Here is the most perfect example I've ever seen. What would it be like if we all acted more like dogs (perhaps we'll leave out the sniffing part) in our relationships? Spend a day sometime trying to act more like a dog and be totally accepting of everyone else's ideas and behavior. You might like it.

## Organizational Cholesterol; The Cardio-Thorasic System Metaphor for Organizational Innovation

The body gives us some great metaphors for organizational behavior. Every organ and system within a body provides the potential for a great dialogue about organizations. They need to be held together by skeletal systems, they need to be nourished, they must grow and reproduce, they need to learn, and their life systems need to be sustained. A real life experience introduced me to the cardio-thorasic system and I found that this system has a tremendous number of commonalties to the process of pumping life into organizations. The heart, lungs, arteries, and veins work constantly to provide life to the body. Oxygenated blood is pumped by the heart through the arteries to the entire body and provides nourishment to cells. It is returned to the lungs to pick up more oxygen and then back to the heart to start the cycle over again. Pretty simple, huh? It is when everything is working right. What is the organizational equivalent of the heart, the arteries, the lungs, the oxygen, and the cells? Organizations also need to have life sustaining knowledge and creative ideas pumped through

172

their bodies if they are to survive and prosper. So why not just emulate the way the cardio-thorasic system works and create its organizational equivalent?

Unfortunately, our organizations, like our bodies, tend to wear out over time. In the cardio-thorasic system a common problem is the build-up of blockages in the arteries. The arteries transferring blood become narrowed with cholesterol deposits and may even become totally blocked. Sometimes small detour arteries are created around the obstruction. Organizations also do a pretty good job of building new roads around blockages. Sooner or later these blockages will manifest themselves as pain when the system can't get the blood flow it needs. In times of high physical or mental stress the body calls for more oxygenated blood and the system can't respond. The result might be pain, an attack, or a stroke. I know lots of organizations that have had the same problems.

What is the organizational equivalent of cholesterol? How do organizations get around blockages and what are the organizational equivalents of these blockages? When we can't get things to flow through normal organizational arteries, what happens? And, what is the significance of this, especially relative to the long-term health of the enterprise?

The main choices you have when there is significant enough blockage within the arteries to cause concern are:

- Live with the pain.
- Displace, or remove, the blockage.
- Create new roads around the blockage.
- Slowly reverse what's causing the blockage.

**Living with the pain.**

This pain is commonly referred to as *angina* and more than a few people, and organizations, live with this pain. This seems like a good short-term option but, unless there is a reversal of whatever is causing the pain in the first place, things will ultimately get worse. The objective here is to stay comfortable by not taking any risks. If your organization is in this category I guarantee there is no innovation. Breakthrough never occurs in the comfort zone.

**Displace, or remove, the blockage.**

A common method, *angio-plasti*, is to push aside the blockage in the arteries. This is suitable only in cases where the blockage is not too severe. A balloon is inflated within the artery at the blockage site and the plaque is pushed against the artery wall with a stint put in place to hold it there. What is the organizational equivalent of this? My guess is that there are many organizational development techniques designed to push blockages out of site, in hopes that they will never return. Guess what? They return! Sooner or later the blockage will again develop at the same site and probably at other sites as well.

**Creating new roads around the system**

In this case, new arteries (borrowed from other parts of the body) are used to by-pass areas of extreme blockage. It's pretty invasive but provides a fairly long-term fix if the cause of the blockage is removed. Would an organizational equivalent of a by-pass operation bring your organization back to health? Are the blockages severe enough to warrant something this invasive? How will you get to the heart of the organization and what major skeletal work must be done? How will you keep the organization alive during the operation? Where will you harvest new arteries for the by-pass? And how will your organization recuperate from the operation?

**Reverse what's causing the problem**

All the options so far suffer from a similar, and critical, problem. If nothing is done to reverse what caused the problem in the first place it will very likely return. Each successive method just gives you a little more time. To be innovative and healthy in the long term requires a healthy lifestyle. What is the organizational equivalent of a heart healthy lifestyle? What should the new, healthy diet of the organization consist of? How might we test for organizational cholesterol and other signs of impending blockage?

There are a lot of powerful questions here. Try out this metaphor in your organization. Maybe some day I'll tell about a lighter metaphor I've been working on – *Organizational Viagra*.

# Do We Really Need Another Survey?

Surveys are for managers that want to know what is going on in their organizations – but are afraid to ask. Okay, that's a pretty harsh statement and I'm sure it's not true all the time. But in my experience I've just seen so many situations where a great deal of money was wasted on surveys when the far better plan would have been to just get out and ask people what they are thinking. After all, in almost all cases, when something is wrong in an organization it has some connection to the state of their inability to communicate. Doesn't it make more sense to forego the survey and begin assessing how people feel by asking them? You'll save money, raise the level of trust, and improve communications all at once.

175

# The Innovation Catch 22

It is very difficult to convince someone that an organization that is experiencing a downsizing needs to consider enhancing his or her innovative capacity. When a company is on the downswing they look at themselves in the survival mode and usually start to shed the innovative capacity that might help bring them back to greatness. I don't know how many times potential clients have told me that they would consider having me work with them to become more creative and innovative as soon as they are *back on their feet*. Once they solve today's problems they will think about developing the tools for more innovative ways to create a great future.

The catch 22 exists because most companies don't think they need to be creative and innovative when things are really going well either. After all, if things are so great why do we need to do anything different? The bottom line is that many organizations shy away from the possibility of being more innovative because they are either too busy solving problems of a poor business climate or basking in the temporary benefits of a good climate. I believe the result of this is the potential of vacillating from good to bad without the opportunity of ever achieving greatness.

## Benchmarking – Staying at the Rear End of Your Competition

I remember back in the late 80's when benchmarking was the hot topic. It seemed like a pretty good idea but there was always something about it that rubbed me the wrong way – and still does. If the ultimate goal of an organization is to keep up with the competition then benchmarking will help. But why would an organization ever be satisfied with this as a goal? I believe that the only benchmarking that is really valuable is *benchmarking the impossible*.

When you create benchmarks of what others are already doing then probably the best you'll do is to catch up with them. If you get aggressive perhaps you'll leapfrog them a bit. Benchmarking will never put you in a position to leave your competition in the dust or to create great breakthroughs. The goal should be to find out what is impossible and then use that as a benchmark. "How can we do things we now think of as impossible?" is a much more powerful question than, "How can we keep up with the competition?". It's also a much more difficult question because you are trying brings thing into view that are in our blind zone. Impossibilities are not readily visible. I hope some of the concepts and techniques in this book will help you to see the opportunities that are not readily visible to you.

## Things I Don't Want to Hear Again

As a speaker I am constantly updating my material so as to keep it unique and fresh. And it personally annoys me to hear other speakers constantly repeating old concepts and stories. The next time I have to listen to the story about the boiling frog, the light house, the ham with its ends cut off, or the number of Eskimo words for snow I'm taking a walk. Likewise if I'm asked to solve the nine dots problem or fold my arms the opposite way. And I don't want to ever hear about the fear of speaking being second to the fear of dying or that Edison invented 14 billion ways not to design a light bulb before he came up with the right one. I refuse to comment on the design of the backward wheelbarrow or re-design a bathtub again.

And there are some things that are so annoying, useless, and silly (like the six thinking hats) that even hearing them once is too

177

much. It's time to bring some really original thinking into the field of original thinking.

## The Innovative Stir-Fry

Thinking about innovation in organizations always brings cooking to my mind. The act of making a sandwich, salad, soup or pasta dish, or a stir-fry is always a great analogy of what goes into the creative/innovative climate. Next time you do some serious cooking or watch a serious cook think about the ingredients, preparation, mixing, stirring, blending, and cooking. What do each of these aspects of cooking suggest about your organization? Pretend you are actually cooking up some great ideas. What are the tools and techniques of a great cook? How do you make sure you have the right ingredients and that they are correctly combined? How do you spice up the whole thing?

If your organization is more like a TV dinner then you've got some work ahead of you.

## The Seasons of Creativity

When I lived in Upstate New York in October I would set aside a day completely devoted to taking in the incredible autumn beauty of the area. I'd jump into my 40 year old TR3A and spend the day driving the hills and valleys in and around our Finger Lakes region. There are few places more beautiful and I do some of my best thinking while driving. I think it has something to do with the purr of the engine coupled with the constantly stimulating visual display. One year while making the trip it occurred to me that the seasons are a very interesting metaphor for creative thinking. Each season provides a different metaphorical twist to our

178

thinking and, when we put these all together, the overall result just might be spectacular. Let's play with this for a while.

Autumn is a time for shedding a lot of the well-rooted, mature ideas that have been adding color to our lives, but are getting tired. The great colors of summer give way to even more spectacular autumn colors. The falling leaves represent our ability to break current thinking patterns and the ultimate composting of these leaves represents the great idea enhancing value that our combined experience and learning gives us. The absence of leaves exposes the wonderful trunk and branch structure of the trees, which gives us a nice metaphor for the backbone of our thinking. If you were a child growing up in a seasonal climate you probably felt compelled to save a few of the more beautiful leaves and this is a good metaphor for building on past idea nuggets. The **autumn season of the mind** is the time to challenge and shed old thinking and get reacquainted with the principles and values that support your thinking. Late autumn brings that first killing frost which ushers us into winter thinking.

Winter is a time for quiet thinking, contemplation, and introspection. As an author I find winter is my best time for writing and for generating some great new creative ideas. Deciduous trees, bulbs, and perennials are storing energy in their roots and gaining strength during the winter because they don't have to *show off* for a few months. A lot of our creative thinking is blocked by our need to *look good* and *show off.* Winter thinking suggests that we think below the surface without worrying about how we will be judged. A blanket of snow just adds a little more security to protect those new, creative, and fragile ideas. As winter wears on, evergreens and the basic structure of trees that became exposed in the autumn can really strut their stuff. Since these are great metaphors for the basic principles and structures that guide our thinking it helps us to stay in touch and build from them. The **winter season of the mind** is the time for understanding the roots of your thinking and internally energizing the seeds of new ideas.

And then comes spring when everything comes to life again. It's also a time for massive cleanup, as any gardener knows. This is when new plants (ideas) really begin to grow and are nurtured along by warmer temperatures, longer days, and rain. We rake, prune, cultivate, fertilize, plant, aerate, and mow because we know that whatever we do now will stick with us for a good part of the year. We also know that it will create healthier roots for new ideas in the future. What are some ways that you and your organization carry out these tasks to help new ideas grow? The **spring season of the mind** is a time for growth and expansion of new ideas.

Summer is a time for harvesting and enjoying the fruits of our labor. For many it means vacation, a time to take your thinking to a more relaxing place and to view it from different perspectives. In winter thinking the energy is concentrated below the surface, at the root level. Summer thinking creates new ideas and expands on what is above the surface. We look at what we have and trim, prune, and deadhead to create more beauty. The **summer season of the mind** is a time for improving and enjoying our ideas.

Enjoy the seasons of your mind, expand on this metaphor and let me know what ideas come to mind. If you are from an area that does not enjoy the different seasons and could make no sense out of any of this, then I apologize to you and sympathize with you.

Well I hope these thoughts have tickled a few of your brain cells. Now let's take a look at one of the key things necessary to create a great future for your organization – how to scout the future.

# Chapter 7

# Scouting the Future

## Scouting the Future of Your Organization; The Process of Strategic Exploration

I am convinced that organizations not only have to tap the creative and innovative minds of their people but also have to put into place methods for creating future pull. Creativity and innovation can flourish when there is a true future mindset. While at Kodak I became intrigued with the teachings of Joel Barker in the late 80's relative to the impact of paradigms on thinking. I had been a long-time member of the World Future Society and very interested in how to make Kodak a future oriented company. I linked up with Joel for a while and that's when I really decided to bring together my thoughts as a futurist and a creative thinker.

While watching a football game a great metaphor for scouting the future came to me. Great quarterbacks have an incredible sense of anticipating where their receivers will be in the future and the ability to perform now so that ball arrives at the perfect spot at the right time. They actually scout the future in their mind before throwing the ball. In a larger sense that's what we must be able to do in business. And that is what this chapter is all about

There are three ways to assure that your business will be around, and healthy, in the next century:

### Achieving and sustaining excellence

You must need to strive to be the best at what you do. But, guess what? Doing this is a matter of survival these days. There just aren't that many out there striving to achieve mediocrity. Achieving excellence will only help you keep up with the other survivors.

## Being innovative

This allows you to get the *"one upsmanship"* you need to stay ahead. The focus is on becoming more interesting (in the eyes of your client) rather than just better. It can, however, result in a never-ending game of *leap frog*.

## Anticipate the future

This is what can really give you a ticket to the future when correctly linked to the right programs for excellence and innovation. It is not only about predicting the future and reacting to it. It's about purposely developing the future that you want by being aware of, anticipating, and creatively building upon information we now have about the future.

In the past few years I have questioned many of my friends and associates from a wide variety of companies to find out what they are doing in the way of futuring processes. I have yet to find any company that has an overt attempt to scout the future. Some companies have strategic planning processes but these are almost always a far cry from what I'm talking about because they focus on pushing today forward. I'm talking about pulling your company to a desirable, breakthrough future – and there's a big difference. Most companies feel that if they pump enough money into research they will make enough discoveries that will turn into moneymaking products. In other words, money plus a good dose of serendipity will get us to the future. It may also get you to "broke". Remember, "A vision without a task is but a dream, a task without a vision is drudgery, a vision and a task is the hope of the world." (1730, a church in Sussex England).

The majority of businesses today are more involved in solving their daily problems than they are in creating a desired future. When you're busy solving problems there is simply no time or energy left to create what you want. All your time is taken seeking relief from your perceived problems. As C.K. Prahalad says in *Competing for the Future*:

"Although strategic planning is billed as a way of becoming more future oriented, most managers, when pressed, will admit that their strategic plans reveal more about today's problems than tomorrow's opportunities."

Successful future scouting must be framed by a clear, shared vision of what you want to become in the future. This vision must be positive, exciting, and provide enough stretch to create a high energy for achievement. Think of a rubber band as an analogy. An un-stretched band just falls to the floor when you let go of it. A well-stretched one really takes off when you let go. One that is stretched too much might break.

The role of benchmarking in the strategic exploration process is worth mentioning. Benchmarking has the potential of supplying some good information but there is a definite downside to this process. In many cases benchmarking is the epitome of being in the problem-solving mode. Let's see what the competition is doing so we can keep up with them. There is a danger of being satisfied that you have kept up with the others when the real task is to achieve breakthroughs that you or your compctititors have never even thought about. Make benchmarking a part of the process if you want to but be sure you focus on benchmarking against possibilities rather than just the current state of things.

# Some *Dos* and *Don'ts* of Strategic Exploration

It's important to pay attention to the people assigned the task of strategic exploration. Ideally they should be a diverse group of "out of the box" thinkers. Nothing very exciting will come from a group that consists of virtual clones from within the organization. You need some rebels – some people that occasionally have spinach hanging from their teeth. Outside influence or talented facilitator with skills in creative thinking techniques can also help. It's best to have a group dedicated to the process and their first job is to create an exiting name for themselves. Forget about the typical corporate group names accompanied by the typical corporate acronyms. Have them give themselves a name that really turns them on. See Appendix K for some job titles that should help trigger some possible group names.

I've mentioned this before but it's worth expanding. While I was Kodak's *creative thinking guru* I linked up with a group of *movers and shakers* within the company who felt that the company wasn't preparing for the future of photography. This was in the late 80's and digital photography was in its infancy. It's rather ironic that Kodak was a key player in its development but the majority of management felt that it would not have a strong impact on silver halide photography. They felt that the traditional photographic process would always have far superior results than what digital would ever provide. Besides that, making film by the mile and selling it by the inch was a huge *cash cow*.

We established a team without management's true blessing and proceeded to take a detailed look at possible futures for photography. We named ourselves the ***Future Innovation Strategies Team*** (or **F.I.S.T.** for short). We designed a logo as well which was a fist smashing down on a pair of dimes

185

(smashing paradigms). We put a lot of hours into developing what we thought would be a very convincing need to expand our digital capabilities right away. When we presented this to key managers they were politely disinterested. It was probably only a couple of years later when the company began its sad downward spiral.

The process used for scouting the future needs to be simple but it also needs to provide some powerful thinking stretches. There's a tendency to create complex processes in organizations that can die of their own weight. The process I outline later in this chapter should be a good starting point but your group's early task is to lay out a process that they are comfortable with.

It is critical to address the issue of how to communicate the results and to assure that appropriate action takes place. After all, the purpose of strategic exploration is to create a breakthrough future for your organization. That won't happen unless the ideas generated are turned into action items. It would be like having a brainstorming session, creating a long list of new ideas, and then not doing anything (which, of course has never happened in your organization).

Strategic exploration can be done at all levels. If you are in the business of human relations, training, research, work systems design, or just about anything, you should be scouting the future of your specialty.

The strategic exploration effort needs to be embodied by an *opportunity mindset* rather than a *threat mindset*. In other words, the process needs to be carried out by people who see *the green near every sand trap* rather than those who see *the sand trap near every green*. They should also have an *attacker* mindset rather than a *defender* one. Richard Foster in his book, *Innovation, the*

*Attacker's Advantage,* builds a very good case as to why the attacker enjoys an advantage over a defender.

## The Strategic Exploration Process

So how do you go about scouting the future for your organization? The following process is based on my own experience and you should feel free to put your own spin on it so it adapts to your own needs. Just remember one thing – keep it simple. I may be repeating myself but. If you insist on making this a complex process, it will die of its own weight. You'll have a lot of fun but they'll never be any useful output. Strategic exploration is a bit like brainstorming – you can do it till the cows come home but, if you lose site of the need for a bottom-line output, it will be a total waste of time. Here's an overview of the process:

- o Prepare the Mindset

- o Gathering the Input

- o Analyzing the Input and Developing Possible Future Scenarios

- o Developing Future Plans and Directions.

Let's take a walk through each of these steps.

## Preparing the Mindset

The purpose of this phase is to prepare those who will be part of the process to think in some different ways. This is often a rather difficult task since, for the most part, we come from a problem solving culture. To achieve the right mindset people need to think in some different ways, see things they have not seen, and do some things that may be uncomfortable.

A good place to begin is to make sure there is a shared vision of the future you want to create. Scouting the future makes little sense if you have no idea where you're going. On the other hand, movement in any direction is often better than no movement at all. I've seen groups get so hung up on describing their future so perfectly that they had no energy left to create it. The visioning may be as simple as asking what you want to create (I think I want to go west– let's take a scouting trip in that direction). Or it may be as complex as using the Strategic Architecture model of C.K. Prahalad and Gary Hammel to describe strategic intent, core platforms, core competencies, leadership disciplines, and organizational arrangements. Again, try to stay on the simple side of this. Define what you want (or think of it as what you want to be when you grow up), call it strategic intent if it makes you feel better, spend a bit of time on defining your core competencies, and then move on. The scouting process will provide you with the momentum you need to keep you going in the direction of your vision.

Sometimes a simple exercise can make a real difference. In the past I have asked groups to brainstorm two questions and put the results on opposite sides of the room. What are the words that people use to describe us today? What are the words that we hope people will use to describe us in the future? Now they have something that is in front of them that describes where they are going.

Another key part of the mindset shifting process is to take a good look at the paradigms that are currently influencing how you think about your business. For those who need a definition of

188

paradigms, they are patterns or rules that we have in our minds about the way things are. These create filters in our thinking which tend to keep us from seeing what is possible. I devoted an entire chapter in my first book, *The Whack-A-Mole Theory*, to this topic because it is so critical to the change process.

The objective is to be able to shift these paradigms but, if you are going to do this, you need to identify them. This is not always easy since, by definition, you are blind to most of them. There is either the best/worst (it's hard to see them) or the worst/worst (you can't see them at all). Joel Barker's video, Discovering the Future; The Business of Paradigms, is a classic in this area and you should see it if you haven't already. It's been around for a long time but is still very applicable.

**Key questions that need to be asked include:**

**What are some paradigms that currently influence the way we see our business?**

I have found it useful to focus these questions in several categories such as:

- Technology
- Research
- Organization
- Environment
- Manufacturing
- Others that suite your needs

What is impossible to do today that, if it were possible, would fundamentally change the way we think? In what areas have we resigned ourselves to settle for less than what is possible?

189

What would others (competition, suppliers, customers, employees, stockholders, and the community) say if asked about our paradigms?

**What are our competitor's paradigms?**

You may also want to spend some time thinking about the things that are currently perceived as threats and ask yourself how it might be different if you were to consider them as great opportunities.

This is hard work and, in my experience, I've found that groups tend not to be able to get into these questions as deeply as they should. You are trying to identify things that you can't see very well (or sometimes not at all). Strong facilitating support using someone from outside your existing thought constraints can make a world of difference. Remember that the idea here is to create some totally different mindsets about what is possible – to make substantial breaks from the thinking that got you to where you are now. If you don't do a great job at this stage you might just as well go back to a problem solving culture and wait for that early retirement opportunity.

## Gathering the Input

This is the fun part – all diverging processes are fun. The purpose of this phase of the scouting process is to identify trends, innovations, paradigm shifts and discontinuities that will have possible implications for your business. Appendix A is loaded with lots of good future stuff. I've done a lot of your scouting work for you here.

The following is a summary I use to help me think about the future. Again, add your own spin to this based on your own knowledge and gut feel. Future opportunities for creativity and innovation in business will come from:

- Future Trends
- Driving Forces
- New Technologies
- Capabilities Derived from New Technologies
- Miscellaneous Stimulators

*Future trends* are things we see happening now, or things we can project, over which we have little or no control. There is a move toward a spike in the older population, many of whom are going to want to grow older in style. Many people will be moving away from the *one career in life* path and cashing out of their jobs to do things they've only fantasized before. We can't control these trends but they sure have many valuable implications for business. There are strong trends towards higher levels of interest in the ecology and consumer manipulation of the marketplace. What do these mean to your business? A good source to start your thinking about future trends is Faith Popcorn's books, *The Popcorn Report* and *Clicking*. There are many other books available through the World Future Society bookstore to help you.

*Driving forces* are characteristics of today's business that we can focus on to help us create new opportunities. Creating speed and convenience for our customers drives us to new innovations in our products. Providing increased customer service and quality will drive us into other areas of innovation. Robert Tucker's book, *Managing the Future* is an excellent starting point for understanding the future drivers. Identify the drivers for your future and use creative thinking techniques to work within each of them to identify new possibilities.

*New technologies* are always a great source for scouting. As a technically oriented futurist I would constantly track these and look for opportunities to find interesting connections of use to my clients. The list of new technologies is long and there are always surprising sources for innovation within them. Here's a short list of emerging technologies. Select a few that might be related to your business. Think of each one as Gretsky's hockey puck. It's moving fast! Where will it be in a few years? If you follow it you'll be too late. How can you cut cross-lots and meet it when it gets there? What direction must you take? How can you get there quickly while conserving resources so you won't be too exhausted to act when you arrive?

- Virtual Reality
- Nanotechnology
- Digital Electronics
- Artificial Intelligence
- Lasers and Optoelectronics
- Fuel Cells
- Thin Film Deposition
- Advanced Expert Systems
- Fuzzy Logic
- Biomimetics
- Materials Science
- Chronobiology
- Genetics
- Fiber Optics
- Superconductors

*New capabilities* are derived from these technologies which provide broad opportunities for innovation. For example, several of these technologies will combine to provide an awesome information highway in the future. What specific implications and opportunities will the existence of this highway have for your business in the future? Now consider these:

- Advanced Storage Media
- Desktop Publishing and "zines"
- Ubiquitous Computing
- Virtual Communities and Corporations
- Digital Interactive TV
- Electronic Notepads
- Homes of the Future

And there are others! Informationalization, as detailed in Stan Davis's book, *2020 Vision,* suggests that a number of opportunities will come from the information within existing products and services. Green marketing and cycle-of-life provide great sources for rethinking products. Enhancing the commonplace will continue to be a lively place to apply creative thinking and innovation. Many products and services that we think of as mature are just waiting for an injection of creative thinking. The world is waiting for someone to reinvent tired old products such as hamburgers, nails, movie theaters, and home appliances. Opportunities abound in re-creating things that have been lost and putting the *fun* back into almost everything.

## Analyzing the Input and Developing Possible Future Scenarios

There are some valuable tools available to help scout the future. *Wheels of implication* help you identify certain key events and examine several levels of resulting events that may have implications that were previously invisible. *Cross impact matrices* provide an opportunity to map relationships between some of the key directions and our strategic objectives. *Growth curve analysis* helps you examine where you are in your cycle of growth and examine the nature of this position. It also helps you to identify the shortcomings involved with your current position on the curve.

*Scenario writing* has been around for a while (1921 to be more exact). In a nutshell, scenarios are narratives of the future. To learn more about this topic I suggest reading *The Art of the Long View* by Peter Schwartz. The process I have used successfully in the past was to ask each team member to write a scenario for a 20 year future of the business. After each scenario is read the team would pick 3-5 that seemed to do the best job of describing possible futures. Based on these, write three scenarios:

- Worst case
- Probable case
- Stretch case.

These stories will be used to identify future plans.

## Developing Future Plans and Directions

It's time to sort it all out and form some specific plans for the future. Based on the material developed from the previous steps what are your recommendations? How are we going to get to the great future that we have envisioned? The more specific and

194

actionable these plans are the higher the probability is that they will be carried out.

I wish you luck. And now let me leave you with some great tips for squeezing your own thinking juices.

# Chapter 8

# How to Be a Raging, Inexorable, Thunder-Lizard, Idea Generator

I hope you've had as much fun reading this book as I've had writing it. I'm hoping that this book instills in all its readers a sense of real excitement as to what is possible when we are able to tap our creative resources. I hope I've left you with some great ideas and a great feeling of optimism that you can make a tremendous difference in whatever you do. This last chapter should put the finishing touches on all this. Its purpose is to get you high on yourself and your capability to make an incredible difference. With the tools and ideas in this book you have the capacity to do things you never thought possible. There are two things needed to enable you to move on to a great future:

♦ Passion
♦ Focused Vision

The need for these two items rings true for individuals as well as organizations but, right now, we are focusing on your own personal creativity. Without them, there is no compelling reason to get excited about the wonderful tips contained in this chapter. If *passion* about what you are doing is totally lacking then, no matter what you do, you will not be able to tap your creative potential. If the charcoals aren't burning there will never be any sizzle in the steak. In general, the higher your passion about your work, the easier it will be for you to achieve breakthrough results. You don't necessarily need *mouth-foaming* passion but you do need a critical mass of it to put you in position to achieve great things. As a matter of fact, too much passion could get in the way. A good amount of passion along with the stimulation from accomplishing great things in your work will put you in an ideal position.

Focused vision is a bit more complex. What it amounts to is having a vivid picture in your mind of what your success looks like. You may also bring in the other senses and add to this what your success *feels*, *sounds*, and even *smells* like. I recently stumbled on a good example of the antithesis of vision which can be illustrated by the first runner-up of Omni Magazine's *New Scientific Theories* contest.

> *If an infinite number of rednecks riding in an infinite number of pickup trucks fire an infinite number of shotgun rounds at an infinite number of highway signs, they will eventually produce the entire world's great literary works in Braille.*

That is not an example of focused vision. It reminds me of what a friend of mine would often tell me, "Even a blind squirrel finds an acorn now and then". Try taking this test before you go to sleep tonight. As you lay there try to bring up a picture in your mind of yourself as the huge success you would like to see. What do you look like? How does it feel? What do you hear? Just try to bring up a vivid picture of this. If you have vision you should be able to do a pretty good job of this and, with practice, you'll be able to fine tune this vision. Now you are ready to go on.

I want to leave you with some tips for doing just that – ten tips for how to be a *raging, inexorable, thunder-lizard idea generator.*

## Tip #1- Be Aware of Your Incredible Creative Capacity

Everyone (you and me included) comes loaded with an incredible capacity for creativity. The problem is that we experience things in our lives that result in a build-up of blockages. Over time these blockages erode our self-confidence so that most people begin to believe that they are just not that creative. Ask your friends and associates if they are creative and you'll find most of them will hedge a bit or just say no. So the first thing I want you to do is to tell yourself that you are incredible creative. Go ahead – do it now. And keep telling yourself until you really, truly believe it. And as you convince yourself of your creative capacity don't forget to throw in the proclamation that you can really make a difference in everything in which you are involved. Remember:

"If you think you're too small to make a difference then you've never been in bed with a mosquito"

Earl Nightingale's #1 secret to life is, "You are what you think". How powerful thought that is. If you think of yourself as being incredibly creative then guess what? You will be incredibly creative!

## Tip # 2 – Loosen Up and Make a Fool of Yourself More Often

The mother of all creative blockages is the fear of failure. Most of us are afraid of failing, are afraid of looking bad, and are afraid of being judged. So we react to this fear by never going out on the limb. Breakthrough never comes when you're standing on safe ground. You can never steal second base if you don't leave first base. To make it a bit worse we live in a world where judgement is the norm. Mention a new and different idea and most often you'll be met with a barrage of comments as to why it can't be done. Westinghouse was labeled an idiot when he suggested using air to stop trains and Alexander Graham Bell was called a fool when he suggested the idea of the telephone. As a matter of fact, most people are pretty good at self-judgement too. How many times have you called yourself an idiot for thinking about some idea that appeared to be foolish? You not only have to cope with negative comments on the part of others – you also have to put up with your own, and often brutal, self-judging thoughts. And sometimes these are so subtle that you don't even know they exist.

It may take some practice to get over this fear and perhaps the best way to do it is to go with the mental bunge jumping idea. Start off some day by telling yourself that you will be spending the day challenging everything and taking everything to the limit. I start many of my workshops by having people make ugly bat faces at each other. After they do that for a while they don't have to worry about not looking good because they've already let themselves go. Concentrate on being accepting and non-judgmental of ideas from your associates. The best way of getting them to accept your ideas may be to become accepting of theirs. And be aware of your own process of judging your thoughts. Whenever you sense that you are acting as a judge of your own creative thinking have a conversation with yourself about it.

And don't get hung up about making mistakes – these are all are just learning experiences. It has been said that, "Victory goes to the player who makes the next-to-last mistake."

## Tip #3 – Practice Creative *Ubuntu*

I've had the privilege of speaking in South Africa on several occasions and one time I was there I brought back a new, and intriguing native word. The word is *ubuntu* and it means *I am because we are*. If I walk into a room and no one recognizes that I'm there then perhaps I'm not there. In other words, things that you do aren't really done until someone acknowledges them. As I thought this over it occurred to me that one of the major limitations in organization creative thinking is the lack of support from others. There are strong NIH (not invented here) behaviors in organizations. People just tend to not support ideas from others, especially if they are really different and creative. Often people who tend to have lots of creative ideas are viewed as almost dangerous. Sometimes the lack of support will even turn into the downright undermining of the idea. I know what you're thinking. "This never happens in my organization and certainly I am always supportive of my associate's ideas." Think about it. And try your best to provide all out support the next time a friend or associate comes to you with a new idea.

Earlier in the book we discussed the climate of curiosity. One of the major needs for this climate is a high level of trust. One of the best ways I can think of to raise the level of trust is to create an atmosphere of total support. Support comes through great listening, verbal and non-verbal acceptance, and an offering of help to take the idea further. Remember – no great idea ever enters the mind through the mouth. Keep the jazz metaphor in mind here and make sure you do a great job of soloing, being a team player, and supporting other soloists.

## Tip #4 – Question Authority and Break the Rules

My children grew up in the 60s generation where bumper stickers that said, *Question Authority*, were plentiful. Unfortunately at that time doing this was really not all that acceptable. You just did as you were told and accepted the thinking of your superiors. Fortunately things have changed and most of us are loosening up and becoming far less rigid.

Being creative and innovation involves breaking the rules of thinking at all levels. Lao Tzu wrote, "To gain knowledge, add something every day. To gain wisdom, get rid of something every day." Creative people have a way of getting un-stuck from the accepted way of thinking about everything they encounter. There's been a lot written lately about how to turn organizations

202

into *learning organizations*. What I'm suggesting is that they first be turned into *unlearning organizations*. Farming is a good metaphor to illustrate this point. Every so often a field needs to be planted with a new and different crop to stimulate the soil for future years. Every so often you need to plough your old ideas into the ground and plant some new stuff. Are you planting new ground in your work?

I've worked with dozens of organizations to help them really think differently about what is possible. There is an incredibly strong tendency to enhance the current thinking patterns in lieu of breaking with the thinking altogether. It is rare that a change agent from within an organization can bring about the type of thinking shifts necessary to create real breakthrough change. This is particularly true these days when many organizations have at least one eye on the downsizing button. So the first step might be to get someone from outside to help slay a few organizational sacred cows and ruffle a bunch of organizational feathers.

Large organizations that have been around for a long time have a particularly tough problem because of their thick *rule books*. This is often referred to as the *tyranny of the installed base*. And the more successful some organizations are, the more rigid they often become which results in tremendous difficulty when change is necessary (which is pretty much all the time by my calculations). IBM, Kodak, Xerox, Hewlett Packard, General Motors are just a few companies that cannot seem to get out of their rigid thinking and they will be (or perhaps already have been) hurt in the long run because of this.

## Tip #5 – Practice Mental Marination

Mozart once said, "When I am, as it were, completely myself, entirely alone, and of good cheer – say traveling in a carriage, or walking after a good meal, or during the night when I cannot sleep; it is on such occasions that my ideas flow best and most abundantly." What were you doing the last time you had a great idea? Most people say they were taking a shower, driving, running or walking, mowing the lawn, or in some form of sleeping. People seem to do some of their best thinking when engaged in a somewhat *mindless* activity. Perhaps we need to provide a work environment that engorges these sorts of activities. The typical work ethic suggests that, if at first you don't succeed, try harder. The creative work ethic might be, if at first you don't succeed, give up!

Great ideas favor a prepared mind that is given the chance to have a few ideas marinating. Think about all the examples in Chapter 2 of new ideas and inventions that appeared as *ahas* from inventors. These people most often had some great ideas incubating and suddenly discovered the creative connections they needed. How might you prepare your mind and set up some conditions to allow for your own mental marination?

## Tip #6 – Find Your Thinkorarium

About a year ago my son and I were on one of our famous upstate New York fall leaf gawking trips. We happen on a place called the Glen Curtiss Museum in Hammonsport, a very picturesque town in the Finger Lakes region. What a great find! Glen Curtiss was one America's most inventive minds and here's a museum full of his inventions. He lived on a hill overlooking Keuka Lake and had a cupola mounted on his house that contained a room he called his thinkorarium. Here's where he went to do his best thinking. Everyone should have one of these.

A thinkorarium doesn't even have to be a place. It could be something you do that tends to bring out the best in your

204

creativity. Einstein liked to become whatever his problem was. Let me ride on that light wave for a while and see what it's like. Bucky Fuller liked to create words (like tensegrety) that created a thinkorarium in his mind. You may find your best thinkorarium is simply letting your mind wander. You just need to find that special place and go there often.

## Tip #7 – Make Friends with Some Un-Clogged Brains

At Nissan Design International in San Diego they go out of the way not to have similar people working together. They call it *hiring in divergent pairs* and think of it as *creative abrasion*. Yet, in the majority of organizations, people are encouraged to think alike. The term NIH (not invented here) is quite common and refers to the mindset that says, "If it didn't come from me (us) then it isn't good."

While at Kodak I facilitated countless ideation session. I would be called upon when someone really needed to stretch the thinking. My only rule was that I had the option of supplying at least two people of my choice for the session. I went out of my way to find people who were as far away from the product, and were as different from the other participants as they could possibly be. And what a difference this made! These implants didn't know the rules so usually they went about suggesting all sorts of crazy ideas. This, in-turn, helped a great deal to stimulate the others into thinking things they perhaps never would have – and the beat went on.

Find ways to involved people in your ideation processes that are completely un-jaded in their thinking. You may even want to get some children involved. Next time you have a hard time solving a problem, ask your kids what they would do. If you don't have any kids then find some.

## Tip #8 – Go Mental Bunge Jumping Often

This is my all-time favorite mental gymnastic. I've probably mentioned it before but it is well worth repeating. You can do it anytime you want and, when done in a group process, it's always a blast. If you do it enough you'll always be able to easily get to the *zone*. It involves stretching your thinking as far as you possibly can using lots of "What if?" questions. Here's a good example.

A group working on traffic safety once asked how they might create telephone poles that disappeared when hit by a vehicle. We all know that's a ridiculous question. You can't make a pole that disappears when hit – that's impossible. So what did they do? They made poles that *kind of* disappeared when hit. They were designed to shear at the base without doing significant damage to the vehicle which, in a sense, disappeared from the scene of the accident. The results of this are seen all along modern highways today and have saved countless lives.

Another example can be seen in the Grand Prizewinner of the Omni Magazine new scientific theories contest.

> *When a cat is dropped it always lands on its feet and when toast is dropped it always lands with the buttered side facing down. Therefore, I propose to strap buttered toast to the back of a cat. When dropped, the two will hover, spinning inches above the ground, probably into eternity. A "buttered-cat array" could replace pneumatic tires on cars and trucks and "giant buttered-cat arrays" could*

206

*easily allow a high-speed monorail linking New York with Chicago.*

Mental bunge jumping gets your thinking to places it's never been and farther out than it would normally go. Then the trick is to find out how to make that impossibility possible which is a lot more fun, and creatively productive, than pushing your way forward from things you know are possible. You owe it to your self to try this out often.

## Tip #9 – Use Metaphors a Lot

Metaphors give us permission to think well outside our normal patterns. You've seen me use a lot of them in this book. If I were to ask you how we might improve our organization your responses would be shaped by your current images of the organization and the rules dictated by what you now know about them. Think about how different the conversation might be if I started by asking you why our organization is like a compost pile. People will quickly judge comments related to the topic if they are thinking in terms of their current image of it. But if they are thinking in terms of a strange metaphor which is now dictating the conversation they have nothing to judge. You simply can't argue with the answers to why your organization is like a compost pile because it's ground you have never covered. Strange metaphors always give safe haven to creative thinking - the stranger the metaphor, the better. And it's pretty much always fun too.

## Tip #10 - Be *Glutton for Funishment* All the Time

I am totally convinced of the need for more humor in the workplace. The general mindset is that fun-work is an oxymoron (like professional wrestling) and that work is supposed to be a painful experience. Why else would you get paid for it? Work is serious business and having fun and seriousness just don't go together. However, there are some businesses that are paving the way and showing that humor can have a great effect on the bottom-line.

At Southwest Airlines their belief is that, "The line between work and fun should be fuzzy." At Rosenbluth Travel they track a *happiness quotient* and have a *Happiness Barometer Team*. At PeopleSoft *having fun* is an official goal and pictures of grinning employees are pinned up all over the hallways. And the CEO of Cognex, a Boston software company, greets new employees with a Three Stooges *Nyuck Nyuck Nyuck* routine. I don't know about you but the CEO of the company I once worked for had his last laugh when he had gas as a child.

Your sense of humor has a positive impact your creativity, your health, your relationships, your learning and much more. And there's a good chance that this ability is vastly under-used. One of the most interesting facts about humor involves the chicken or egg question, "Are you laughing because you're happy or are you happy because you're laughing?" And it turns out that it can go either way. If you smile or laugh for no particular reason at all, you'll stiff feel good. So don't wait for someone like Robin Williams to appear in your workplace –be your own Robin Williams.

Go out of your way to smile, laugh, cajole, use happy words, be silly, and use all the forms of spontaneous humor you can. It will make a tremendous difference in everything you do. It's quite contagious and it's a disease they most people might enjoy catching.

## Tip#11 – Create Future Pull and Beam Yourself Up Frequently

"I skate to where the puck is going to be, not to where it is". These words from Wayne Gretsky are worth repeating. A day rarely goes by when I don't spend some time reading various books and magazines and noting some future technology, trend, or shift. And this invariably provides me with an exciting rush about new, creative possibilities. A friend of mine once said that the best way to see the future is to go as far as you can – and then look again.

The last chapter covered my own current thinking as to how to scout the future. My hope is that I have given you some exciting and usable ideas that will help you create a wonderful future for yourself and your organization. If I can ever provide you help and guidance along the way, or just provide some applause for you, please don't hesitate to get in touch. I'd love to hear from you at lindsaycollier@comcast.net. Check out my Amazon author site at amazon.com/author/lindsaycollier. Also check out my website (which I call my *thinkorarium*) at lindsaycollier.weebly.com. I look forward to sharing my knowledge of creativity, innovation, and change on this site.

Good luck!

# Appendix A

# Future TIPS
# (Trends, Innovations, and Paradigm Shifts)

"It's a question of whether we're going to go forward into the
future or past to the back."
Vice President Dan Quayle

The following are forces I feel will be shaping our future. These
change rapidly. First are the **trends which will shape the future**.
These are going to happen and you have little control over them.
The trick is to find their implications to you and do something
about it.

| | |
|---|---|
| Concern for ecology | Security and safety |
| Enjoying life | New levels of education |
| Shifting family values | Intellectual property |
| Beautiful aging | Spirit in the workplace |
| Valuing diversity | Globalization |
| Accepting technology | Third world markets |
| Quantum theory | New concepts of work |
| Virtual organizations | Multiple careers |
| Strategic alliances | Socially responsibility |
| Villages re-discovered | Age waves |
| Information society | |

Here are a few **technologies to watch carefully**. Which ones
relate to your business? Pick a few they, at first blush, have no
relationship and find some connections.

211

Virtual reality
Nano technology
Digital electronics
Artificial intelligence
Lasers and optoelectronics
Advanced flat panel displays
Photovoltaic cells
Biotechnology
Robotics
Voice recognition
Fractals
3 D imaging, Holography
Fuel cells
Kenaf
Semi and superconductors
Fiber optics
Pheromones and VNO
Hybrid fuel vehicles
Smart manufacturing
Data storage

Thin film deposition
Advanced expert systems
Fuzzy logic
Neural networks
Diamond thin films
Biomimetics
Photonics
Super materials
Gene pharming
Chronobiology
Genetics
Renewable energy
Environmental technologies

Parallel processing
Tissue engineering/ limb generation
Bio prospecting
Global positioning systems
Digital video disks (DVD

And from these technologies come some **emerging capabilities**. How might these impact you?

Information highway
Internet
Electronic notepads - PIM's
Edutainment
Shop at home
Advanced CD's
Digital interactive TV
Desktop publishing/"Zines"
Ubiquitous computing
Virtual communities/corporations

Home of the future
E-Money
Limb, joint, skin generation
Green markets
New imaging capabilities
Synthetic travel
Symbiotic communities
Foodaceuticals
Smart manufacturing
Hybrid vehicles

"The factory of the future will have only two employees, a man and a dog. The man will be there to feed the dog. The dog will be there to keep the man from touching the equipment."

# Appendix B

# A few of my favorite quotations

(For more see my Kindle book, *Quotations to Tickle Your Brain*)

Use these quotations in a number of ways:

- Post them on walls at meetings
- Pass them out on index cards at meetings and have people introduce themselves by reading and discussing theirs.
- Take time out at meetings and pick one randomly and discuss its meaning to your group and your situation.
- Give people several quotations to think about as homework.
- Have people draw a picture of the quotation.
- Use as a warm-up by having people rotate around the room with their quotation attached to their body to provide discussion material.
- Pick a quotation as a group motto.
- Ask if others have favorite quotations.
- Make up a quotation that is customized for your group.
- Make up silly quotations or pick some and make them silly.


1. It's never too late to have a happy childhood.

2. You are only young once - but you can be immature all your life.

3. Don't be afraid to take a big step if it's needed. You can't cross a chasm in two small jumps.

4. Life is like being on a dog sled team.  If you ain't the lead dog the scenery never changes.

5. A diamond is just a piece of coal that stuck to the job.

6. If in the last few years you haven't discarded a major opinion or acquired a new one then check your pulse - you may be dead.

7. Once you have taken the impossible into your calculations, its possibilities become potentially limitless.

8. You can't always depend on expert opinion.  A turkey, if you ask the turkey, should be stuffed with grasshoppers, grit and worms.

9. The road to success is always under construction.

10. Do not take life too seriously - you will never get out of it alive.

11. To know what to ask is already to know half.  (Aristotle)

12. Carve a person's faults in sand, their accomplishments in stone.

13. If the roof doesn't leak, the architect hasn't been creative enough. (Frank Lloyd Wright)

14. Once a new technology runs over you, you are not part of the steamroller; you are part of the road.

15. It's better to build a fence at the top of the cliff than a hospital at the bottom. (Ann Landers)

16. The best way to predict the future is to invent it. (Alan Kay)

17. You can't build a reputation on what you're going to do. (Henry Ford)

18. Verbal diarrhea is created by people who make vowel movements consonantly.

19. If you torture data sufficiently, it will confess to anything. (Fred Menger)

20. Optimists see an opportunity in every problem. Pessimists see a problem in every opportunity.

21. Seek simplicity - then distrust it. (Alfred North Whitehead)

22. Everywhere you trip is where the treasure lies. (Warren Bennis)

23. If we think more about failing at what we are doing than about doing it, we will not succeed. (Warren Bennis)

24. Everything should be made as simple as possible, but not simpler. (Albert Einstein)

25. The winner sees a green near every sand trap. The loser sees a sand trap near every green.

26. The world that we have made, as a result of the level of thinking we have done thus far, creates problems that we

cannot solve at the same level at which we create them. (Albert Einstein)

27. The things that got you to where you are today are not the things that will get you to the future. (Peter Drucker)

28. Conception is easier than birth - and a good deal more pleasant too.

29. Never underestimate the unimportance of everything. (Steve Allen Jr.)

30. No great idea ever entered the mind through the mouth.

31. Be what you is, not what you ain't - cause if you is what you ain't, you ain't what you is. (Luther D. Price -jazz musician)

32. People who are always raising the roof usually don't have much in the attic.

33. A river is like intelligence - the deeper it is the less noise it makes.

34. No snowflake in an avalanche feels responsible.

35. A ship in harbor is safe - but that is not what ships are for. (John Shedd)

36. It usually takes me at least 3 weeks to prepare a good impromptu speech. (Mark Twain)

37. Only mediocre people are always at their best. (Somerset Maugham)

38. Intelligent people, when assembled into an organization, will tend toward collective stupidity. (Karl Albrecht)

39. Nothing would be done at all if a man waited until he could do it so well that no one could find fault with it. (Cardinal Newman)

40. When in doubt, I tell the truth. (Mark Twain)

41. A vision without a task is but a dream, a task without a vision is drudgery, a vision and a task is the hope of the world. (1730, a church in Sussex England)

42. Anyone who can spell a word only one way is an idiot. (WC Fields)

43. An optimist sees an opportunity in every calamity; a pessimist sees a calamity in every opportunity.

44. Some people never hear opportunity knock because they are too busy knocking opportunity. (Hal Chadwick)

45. What great thing would you attempt if you knew you could not fail. (Robert Schuler)

46. Just because everything is changed doesn't mean anything is different. (Alfred E. Neuman)

47. It is difficult to predict, especially about the future. (Peter Drucker)

48. Do not fear mistakes, there are none. (Miles Davis)

49. Good judgment comes from experience, experience comes from bad judgment. (Tom Watson - IBM)

50. Businesses 3 worst enemies are thinking too big, thinking too small and thinking too much.

51. It takes a long time to grow young. (Picasso)

52. You miss 100% of the shots you don't take. (Wayne Gretsky)

53. I skate to where the puck is going to be, not to where it is. (Wayne Gretsky)

54. Things may come to those who wait, but only the things left by those who hustle. (Abraham Lincoln)

55. Think left and think right and think low and think high. Oh the thinks you can think up if only you try. (Dr. Seuss)

56. A bird does not sing because it has an answer. It sings because it has a song. - Yurok Indian

57. When your heart speaks take good notes. (Yurok Indian)

58. Angels can fly because they take themselves lightly.

59. If the earth had waited for a precedent, it never would have turned on its axis. (Maria Mitchell, astronomer)

60. You are only as good as you dare to be bad. (Timothy Hutton)

61. You can really see a lot by observing. (Yogi Berra)

62. To create you must first destroy. (Picasso)

63. Any significantly advantaged technology is indistinguishable from magic.

64. Next time your mind wanders follow it around for a while. (Lindsay Collier)

65. A new idea is first condemned as ridiculous and then dismissed as trivial, until finally it becomes what everyone knows. (William James)

66. Faced with the choice between changing one's mind and proving there is no need to do so, most people get busy on the proof. (J.K. Galbraith)

67. If I give you a dollar and you give me a dollar we each have a dollar. If I give you an idea and you give me an idea we each have two ideas.

68. Two roads diverged in the wood and I took the one less traveled by, and that has made all the difference. (Robert Frost)

69. Get your facts first, then you can distort them as much as you please. (Mark Twain)

70. If you lose the power to laugh you lose the power to think. (Clarence Darrow)

71. If you have always done it that way, it is probably wrong. (Charles Kettering)

72. Things will get better - despite our efforts to improve them. (Will Rogers)

73. If the parts don't fit the theory - change the theory. (Albert Einstein)

74. Learn the infield fly rule. This will give you a good perspective on life. (Forest Gump)

75. If you think you're too small to be effective you have never been in bed with a mosquito. (Bette Reese)

76. In order to make an omelet you have to break a few eggs.

77. Sometime trying to tune up the old engine is like putting lipstick on a pig. (EDS executive)

78. In the race to the future there are passengers, drivers, and road kill. (C.K. Prahalad)

79. Organizational change is like dancing with a gorilla. You don't stop when you get tired; you stop when the gorilla gets tired.

80. When one door closes, another one opens somewhere.

81. Not everything that matters can be measured, and not everything that can be measured matters. (Albert Einstein)

82. If you don't change your direction you'll likely end up where you're going. (Chinese proverb)

83. Be the change you are trying to create. (Gandhi)

84. You usually don't drown in the sea, you drown in a puddle.

85. Anyone who thinks they're indispensable should stick a finger in a bowl of water and notice the hole it leaves when it's pulled out. (Harvey Mackay)

86. Nothing is less productive than to make more efficient what should not be done at all. (Peter Drucker)

87. Every right idea, no matter how good it is, is eventually the wrong idea. (Peter Drucker)

88. A cow chip is a picnic to a fly. (Texas Bix Bender)

89. We're all in this alone. (Lily Tomlin)

90. Thunder is good. Thunder is impressive. But it's the lightning that does the work. (Mark Twain)

91. Better to remain silent and be thought a fool than to speak up and remove all doubt. (Abraham Lincoln)

92. Reality is for people who lack imagination. - seen on a bumper sticker

93. I am not young enough to know everything. (Little Zen Companion)

94. Whether you believe you can or believe you can't, you're absolutely right. (Henry Ford)

95. The "silly question" is the first intimation of some totally new development. (Alfred North Whithead)

96. Many ideas grow better when transplanted into another mind than in the one where they sprung up. (Oliver Wendell Holmes)

97. When companies try to encourage creativity it's like a bear dancing with an ant. Sooner or later the ant will realize it's a bad idea, although the bear might not. (Scott Adams -Dilbert)

98. Every great oak was once a nut that stood its ground.

99. Managers can't demand creativity any more than they can order growth from a flower. (John Kao)

100. The illiterate of the 21$^{st}$ century will not be those who cannot read or write, but those who cannot learn, unlearn, and relearn. (Alvin Toffler)

# Appendix C

# The Museum of
# Bonehead Remarks

I have spent years collecting these remarks to prove to myself that paradigm paralysis is alive and well in organizations. Enjoy them – and learn from them.

*Stocks have reached what looks like a permanently high plateau.*

Economics, Yale University, 1929Irving Fisher, Professor of

*I think there's a world market for about 5 computers.*

Thomas Watson, IBM. 1943

*There is no reason for any individual to have a computer in their home. The personal computer will fall flat on its face in business.*

Ken Olson, DEC, 1977

*But what is it good for?*

Engineer at Advanced Computer Systems Division of IBM, 1968, commenting on the microchip

*640K ought to be enough for anybody.*

Bill Gates, 1981

*Inventions have long since reached their limit and I see no hope for further development.*

Julius Sextus Frontinus, a highly respected engineer in Rome, 1st century AD

*Everything that can be invented has been invented.*

- Charles Duell, Director of US Patent Office, 1899

*Hey, we don't need you. You haven't even gone to college yet.*

HP's statement to Steve Jobs when he tried to get them interested in his and Steve Wozniak's personal computer

*People will soon get tired of staring at a plywood box every night.*

Daryl Zanuck, 20th Century Fox on the idea of a TV

*We don't like their sound. Besides, guitar music is on the way out.*

President of Decca Records on turning down the Beatles in 1962

*All this concern about auto safety. It's of the same order as the hula hoop - a fad. Six months from now we'll probably be on another kick.*

W.B. Murphy, president, Campbell Soup Company

*You will never amount to much.*

Munich schoolteacher to Albert Einstein when he was
about 10 years old

*The phonograph is of no commercial value.*

Thomas Edison, remarking on his own invention to his
assistant, 1880

*The Japanese auto industry is not likely to carve out a big slice of the
US market.*

Business Week, 1958

*Mr. Ford, I don't think that what we are being offered here is worth
a damn.*

Ernest Breech, Ford CEO on the free offer to take over
VW after the war

*I'm just glad it will be Clark Gable who's falling on his face and
not Gary Cooper.*

Gary Cooper on turning down the leading role in Gone
With the Wind

*Sensible and responsible women do not want to vote.*

President Grover Cleveland, 1905

*Everyone should be quite satisfied with carbon paper.*

Results of a study by AD Little for Xerox on the possible
interest in their new copying invention

*Your game is too complicated and takes too long to play. People will
get bored with it.*

Parker Brothers when turning down Mr. Darrow's new
board game, Monopoly

*Americans require a restful quiet in the moving-picture theater.
Talking on the screen destroys the illusion. Devices for projecting the
film actor's speech can be prefaced, but the idea is not practical.*

Thomas Edison, inventor of the motion picture in the New
York Times, 1926

*Where a calculator on the ENIAC is equipped with 18,000 vacuum
tubes and weighs 30 tons, computers of the future may have only
1,000 vacuum tubes and perhaps weigh 1 1/2 tons.*

Popular Mechanics, forecasting the relentless march of
science, March 1949

*I find it difficult to believe that the seat belt can afford the driver any great amount of protection over and above that which is available to him through the medium of the safety -type steering wheel if he has his hands on the wheel and grips the rim sufficiently tight to take advantage of its energy absorption properties and also takes advantage of the shock-absorbing action which can be achieved by correct positioning of the feet and legs.*

Howard Gandelot, safety engineer for GM, 1954

*This car is ugly, noisy, outlandish, and unsalable.*

The British as they turned down the opportunity of taking over the VW plant.

*The laser has no relevance to the telephone industry.*

Bell Laboratory patent Lawyers

*I have traveled the length and breadth of this country and talked with the best people. I can assure you that data processing is a fad that won't last out the year.*

The editor in charge of business books for Prentice Hall, 1957

*This thing you call a telephone has too many shortcomings to be seriously considered as a means of communication. The device is inherently of no value to us.*

Western Union internal memo, 1876

*A cookie store is a bad idea. Besides, the market research reports say America likes crispy cookies, not soft and chewy like you make.*

Response to Debbi Fields' idea of starting Mrs. Fields''
Cookies

*You want to have consistent and uniform muscle development across all of your muscles? It can't be done. It's just a fact of life. You just have to accept inconsistent muscle development as an intolerable condition of weight training.*

Response to Arthur Jones, who solved the "unsolvable"
problem by inventing Nautilus

*The wireless music box has no imaginable commercial value. Who would pay for a message sent to nobody in particular?*

David Sarnoff's associates in response to his urgings for
investment in the radio in the 1920's

*The concept is interesting and well-formed, but in order to earn better than a "C", the idea must be feasible.*

A Yale University management professor in response to
Fred Smith's paper proposing reliable overnight delivery
service. (Smith went on to found Federal Express Corp.)

*You ain't goin' nowhere, son. You ought to go back to drivin' trucks.*

Jim Denny, Manager of the Grand Ole Opry, after he fired
Elvis Presley after just one performance

*Who the hell wants to hear actors talk?*

H.M. Warner, Warner Brothers, 1927

*Speaking movies are impossible. It will never be possible to
synchronize the voice with the picture.*

D.W.Griffith, filmmaker

*Radio has no future. Heavier-than-air flying machines are
impossible. X-rays will prove to be a hoax.*

Lord Kelvin, British mathematician, physicist, and
president, British Royal Society, 1895

*If I had thought about it, I wouldn't have done the experiment. The
literature was full of examples that said you can't do this.*

Spencer Silver on the work that led to the unique
adhesives for "Post-It" Notepads

*Professor Goddard does not know the relation between action and
reaction and the need to have something better than a vacuum against*

*which to react. He seems to lack the basic knowledge ladled out daily in high schools.*

1921 New York Times editorial about Robert Goddard's revolutionary rocket work

*The wireless music box has no imaginable commercial value. Who would pay for a message sent to nobody in particular?*

David Sarnoff's associates response to his urgings for investment in the radio in the 1920s

*Drill for oil? You mean drill into the ground to try and find oil? You're crazy.*

Drillers who Edwin Drake tried to enlist to his project to drill for oil in 1859

*Airplanes are interesting toys but of no military value.*

Marechal Ferdinand Foch, Professor or Strategy, Ecole Superieure de Guerre, 1911

*Louis Pasteur's theory of germs is ridiculous fiction.*

Pierre Pachet, Professor of Physiology at Toulouse, 1872

*The abdomen, chest, and brain will forever be shut from the intrusion of the wise and humane surgeon.*

Sir John Eric Ericksen, British surgeon, appointed Surgeon-Extraordinary to Queen Victoria, 1873

*Women on certain jobs are every bit as good as men. For instance, we wouldn't think of having a man sell brassieres.*

Drummond Bell, Montgomery Ward vice president

*Man will never reach the moon regardless of all future scientific advances.*

Lee DeForest, New York Times, 1957

*Space travel is utter bilge.*

Sir Richard Van Der Riet Wooley, The Astronomer Royal (1956)

*I am tired of this thing called science. We have spent millions in that sort of thing and it should be stopped.*
Senator Simon Cameron demanding that funding be ended for the Smithsonian Institute, 1861

*Rail travel at high speeds is not possible because passengers, unable to breathe' would die of asphyxia.*

Dionysis Lardner, English scientist, 1793-1859)

*While theoretically and technically television may be feasible, commercially and financially I consider it an impossibility.*

232

Lee deForest, American inventor, (1873-1961)

*The actual building of roads devoted to motor cars is not for the near future, in spite of many rumors to that effect.*

*Harper's Weekly*, 1902

*The bomb will never go off, and I speak as an expert in explosives.*

Vanevar Bush's comment to President Truman regarding the atom bomb

*The flying machine will eventually be fast; they will be used in sport, but they are not to be thought of as commercial carriers.*

Octave Chanute, aviation pioneer, proclaimed in 1904

*The ordinary "horesless carriage" is at present a luxury for the wealthy; and, although its price will probably fall in the future, it will never come into as common use as a bicycle.*

The Literary Digest, 1889

*The cinema is little more than a fad. It's canned drama. What audiences really want to see is flesh and blood on the stage.*

Charlie Chaplin, circa 1916

*Face it, Louis Civil War pictures have never made a dime.*

Irving Thalberg, MGM producer, advising his boss against buying the right for *Gone With the Wind*.

*Just as certain as death, George Westinghouse will kill a customer within six months after he puts in a system of any size.*

Thomas Edison in their ongoing AC vs. DC dispute

*It is, of course, altogether valueless ........ Ours has been the first, and will doubtless be the last, party of whites to visit this profitless locality.*

Lt. Joseph C. Ives, Corps of Topographical Engineers, commenting in 1861 on the future of the Grand Canyon

*I have traveled the length and breadth of this country and talked with the best people in business. I can assure you on the highest authority that data processing is a fad that won't last out the year.*

An editor of business books at Prentice-Hall rejecting a manuscript on data processing, 1957

*Landing and moving around on the moon offers so many serious problems for human beings that it may take science another 200 years to lick them.*

Science Digest, 1948

*That the automobile has practically reached the limit of its development is suggested by the fact that during the past year no improvements of a radical nature have been introduced.*

Scientific American, January 2, 1909

*Well informed people know it is impossible to transmit the voice over wires and that were it possible to do so, the thing would be of no practical value.*

Editorial in the *Boston Post*, 1865

*The telephone has too many shortcomings to be seriously considered as a means of communication. The device is inherently of no value to us.*

Western Union internal memo, 1876

*The worldwide potential for plain a paper copier is less than 5000 units.*

Advice from a major consulting firm to IBM on whether to accept Haloids's offer to acquire their technology

*There is no possibility that man will ever tap the power of the atom.*

Nobel Prize winner Robert Milliken in 1920

*It is an idle dream to imagine that automobiles will take the place of railways in the long distance movement of passengers.*

American Road Congress, 1913

*Wellington is a bad general. We will settle this before lunch.*

Napoleon to his generals

*The talking picture will not supplant the regular silent picture.*

Thomas Edison, 1913

*He possesses minimal football knowledge and lacks motivation.*

An expert referring to Vince Lombardi, famous football coach

*Though import cars sales could hit 425,000 in 1959, they may never go that high again.*

*Business Week*, January 17, 1958

*Nothing has come along that can beat the horse and buggy.*

Chauncey Depew, president of New York central Railroad, warning his nephew against investing in Ford

*Babe Ruth made a big mistake when he gave up pitching.*

Tris Speaker, 1921

*The odds are that the United States will not be able to honor the 1970 manned lunar landing date set by President Kennedy.*

New Scientist, April 30, 1964

*Flight by machines heavier than air is impractical and insignificant, if not utterly impossible.*

Simon Newcomb, a well known astronomer, 1902

*Can't dance. Can't act. Can sing a little.*

Notes from Fred Astair's screen test

*This fellow Charles Lindbergh will never make it. He's doomed.*

Harry Guggenheim, millionaire aviation enthusiast

*If excessive smoking actually plays a role in the production of lung cancer, it seems to be a minor one.*

Dr. W.C. Heuper of the National Cancer Institute, New York Times, April 14, 1954

*With regard to the electric light, much has been said for and against it, but I think I may say without contradiction that when the Paris*

*Exhibition closes, electric light will close with it, and no more will be heard of it.*

Erasmus Wilson, Oxford Professor, 1899

*This fellow Charles Lindbergh will never make it. He's doomed.*

Harry Guggenheim, millionaire aviation enthusiast

*The horse is here to stay, but the automobile is a novelty - a fad.*

The President of the Michigan Savings Bank advising Henry Ford's lawyer not to invest in the Ford Motor Company in 1893

*For the majority of people, smoking has a beneficial effect.*

Dr. Ian G. McDonald, Los Angeles surgeon, Newsweek, Nov 8, 1963

*They'll never replace the steam locomotive.*

A Baldwin Locomotive Company executive

*The PC will never amount to anything but a toy.*

Ken Olson, Digital Equipment Corporation CEO

*Whatever happens, the US Navy is not going to be caught napping.*

Frank Knox, US Secretary of the Navy, on December 4,
1941

*I'm sorry, Mr. Kipling, but you just don't know how to use the English language.*

A San Francisco Examiner editor turning down Kipling's article

*What use would this company make of an electric toy?*

Carl Orton, president of Western Union, to Alexander Graham
Bell, who offered all rights
to the telephone for $10,000

*What on earth would ordinary people do with computers?*

HP's response to Steve Wozniak's idea of a PC (He worked for
them at the time and
felt he had to give them the first opportunity.)

# Appendix D

## Tips for being creative all the time

1. Create a stretch vision of what you want.

2. Try your best to be non-judgmental.

3. Start from outrageous and work back. Practice mental bungie jumping.

4. Examine and upset your thinking patterns often.

5. Break the rules.

6. Seek advice from others - especially those outside your expertise.

7. Wonder a lot and let your ideas and thoughts marinate.

8. If at first you don't succeed - give up - let go.

9. Think in metaphors as much as you can.

10. Laugh a lot and never lose touch with your sense of humor.

# Appendix E

# Design of Creativity and Humor Rooms

The majority of work areas are designed to be either very functional or to look good. Creative thought doesn't tend to flourish in the typical sterile environment that fits these characteristics. Often people just need a place to escape to that allows them to just get outside of their normal thinking box. A number of organizations that I know of have created various designs for creativity or humor rooms. Kodak, John Deere, Ford, Hoechst Celanese are examples. I was the main driver behind the development of the Kodak Humor and Creativity Room in 1991. Let me share with you some of our thinking and a bit about its development.

Why a humor and creativity room?

- It provides a place for people to go to think differently and to find creative connections.
- It's a place for people to develop ideas and to enhance their creativity and humor to enable them to be more effective in their work.
- It's a place for reducing the stress of everyday work.
- It provides an opportunity for networking and sharing ideas and making connections between different thought communities.
- People are given the opportunity to lighten up, smile, and go back to their jobs with new perspectives.
- It creates an ideal and inexpensive area for group ideation sessions.

- It's a symbol that the organization is willing to extend its thinking into new areas. A sign that they are ready to explore possibilities and create breakthrough.

In short, it's a place to get charged, recharged, excited, stimulated, humored, challenged, unstressed, turned on, and transformed. The important thing is to maintain a consistent connection between the work of the organization and the activities of the room. The room should exist for the purpose of building the creative capability of associates and its eventual enhancement of the work they do.

The room needs to be a totally different environment from the normal. The original design of our Kodak Humor Room called for entrance through a hall of mirrors. Our thought was that this would change you to a different person as you entered. Although our budget didn't allow us to do this, everything we did do was an effort to make it different. We took out the false ceilings and overhead lighting that was in just about ever other office location and this alone made a dramatic difference. Bill Cosby, the Three Stooges, and a lot of pretty strange posters replaced pictures of George Eastman (the founder of Kodak). Furniture was an eclectic mix of second hand couches, chairs, and various art deco we collected from various sources. And we went out of our way to stay away from the typical neat office layouts. Although the room wasn't clearly sectionalized, there were four major themes.

The library area had a fairly large selection of books and tapes and some comfortable couches to sit in while browsing. There was no staff in the room. People were asked to not take things from the room and on their honor to return them if they did. Paper and chart pads were there for people to make notes and our plans were to have a small copier available as well. Books included many useful publications on creative thinking along with a large

242

selection of cartoons such as the *Farside* series. I would guess there were about two hundred books all together.

The presentation area had some comfortable seats for a couple dozen people and the audio and video capability so we could play music, laugh tracks, comic routines, or various videos. Videos included Monty Python, Candid Camera, old time movies, and some serious creativity ones. We had a schedule of events published each week. There were also presentations from time to time on topics of interest regarding creativity and humor. The room was frequently used by groups engaging in ideation sessions and it created a great environment for this.

We had the high tech section with a couple of PC's which were loaded with creativity and humor processing software. This wasn't as successful as I had anticipated in part because people didn't have time to learn how to use the software. The intention was to eventually have some training session for those who were interested but that never quite got off the ground.

And the fourth area was what we called our toy store. This included a substantial collection of items - some were in a particular section of the room and some scattered about the room. Items such as:

- spare body parts
- toys
- games
- hats (for viewpoint shifting)
- stress dolls
- punching bags
- silly items (such as laughing bags)
- mind teasers

- catalogues (for idea stimulating)
- animals and other objects
- objects for juggling (balls, scarves, hamburgers, chain saws etc.)

We located a number of easels around the room and suggested certain ideas for these such as quotations, creative ideas for work, jokes, stories and other things for people to share. We also had some that were there for group problem solving. Someone would write down a problem or opportunity and people would write down ideas they had. The thing that perhaps stood out the most in the room was the old commode that some one found and dragged in. Apparently they felt that some of their best thinking took place there. So we put it in a corner of the room right under our collection of hats. When the NBC Today program highlighted the room they showed one of our maintenance associates sitting on the thinking commode wearing a raccoon skin hat. I was skating on some pretty thin ice with some of the execs after that one.

# Appendix F

# Biography of Readings on Creativity and Innovation

When I first became interested in creativity and innovation there were only about three books on the topic. Now there are hundreds! The following are the ones that I would recommend because they have been very helpful to me. Each of them expands the thinking on the topic of creativity rather than just re-hashing old thoughts and techniques. I've taken the liberty of expressing my own personal thoughts about each one to help you choose from a long list of possibilities.

Adams, James, *Conceptual Blockbusting*, WW Norton, 1979 – An oldie but goodie.

Adams, James, *The Care and Feeding of Ideas*, Addison Wesley, 1986 – Not as good as his first one.

Barker, Joel, *Future Edge*, William Morrow, 1992 - A good look at how to explore the future.

Black, Robert Alan, *Broken Crayons*, Kendall/Hunt, 1995 - Alan is a good friend of mine and I like everything nice people like him do.

Collier, Lindsay, *Get Out of Your Thinking Box*, RL Reed Publishing, 1994 - Lots of fun and laughs – you can't stop reading it.

Collier, Lindsay, *The Whack-A-Mole Theory*, WhAM Books, 1996 -Okay, I'm bias. But people have told me that this is one of the most straightforward books on organizational breakthrough ever.

Collier, Lindsay, *Quotations to Tickle Your Brain*, Kindle/Nook books, June 2013 - Not the biggest collection – only the best!

Collier, Lindsay, *Organizational Braindroppings, Musings on Organizational Breakthrough and Change*, Kindle/Nook books, June, 2013 – A collection of articles I've written for various publications, Short, different, and fun!

Collier, Lindsay, *The Meaning of Life* - Okay, I admit, there is no such book. But maybe someday!

Csikszentmihalyi, Mihaly, *Creativity*, Harper Perennial, 1996 – This book is almost as hard to read as the author's last name.

Davis, Rick, *Totally Useless Office Skills*, Hobblebush Books, 1996 – This will bring out the *strange* in you!

Davis, Stan, *2020 Vision*, Fireside, 1991 – One of my favorites! Oldie but goody (just like me)

DeBono, Edward, *Six Thinking Hats*, Little Brown & Co., 1985 – Some people seem to like this. I'm not sure why because I think it's pretty dumb.

DeBono, Edward, *Lateral Thinking* – Some people think of this as a classic. I think of it as the only good book he has ever written.

DePree, Max, *Leadership Jazz*, Currency Doubleday, 1992 – Worth reading if you have some extra time.

Dr. Seuss, *Oh the Thinks You Can Think*, Random House, 1975 – You should read this once a week!

Drucker, Peter, *Innovation & Entrepreneurship*, Harper & Row, 1986 – An incredible piece of work, as most of his books are. Another oldie but goodie.

Edwards, Betty, *Drawing on the Right Side of the Brain*, Jeremy Tarcher, 1979 – One of my first creative thinking books. Full of great ideas and ranks as one of the best in the *oldies but goodies* class. Her ideas don't get old.

Edwards, Betty, *Drawing on the Artist Within*, Fireside Books, 1987 – Follow-ups are never as good as the original.

Fahden, Allen, *Innovation on Demand*, The Illiterati, 1993 – An enjoyable book with a few good twists on the topic.

Flatlow, Ira, *They All Laughed*, Harper Collins, 1992 – A fun read full of stories about various inventions of out time.

Foster, Richard, *Innovation*, Summit Books, 1986 – A definite classic that should be read by everyone.

Freiberg, Kevin, *Nuts*, Bard Press, 1996 – A great story about that crazy outfit called Southwest Airlines and how they proved that the funny line and the bottom line can intersect.

Fritz, Robert, *The Path of Least Resistance*, Still Point, 1984 – Another classic! This book will never grow old.

Fritz, Robert, *Creating*, Fawcett Columbine, 1991 – Pretty good as follow-ups go.

Gawain, Shakti, *Creative Visualization*, Bantam Books, 1978 – Pretty good stuff if you like floating around in pink balloons.

Gelb, Michael, *How to Think Like Leonardo da Vinci*, Delacorte Press, 1998 – Some pretty unique thoughts on creative thinking.

Hall, Doug, *Jump-Start Your Brain*, Warner Books, 1995 – I really enjoyed this. You can tell he probably writes in his bare feet.

Hawken, Paul, *Growing a Business*, Fireside, 1987 – A gem in the woods. Don't miss it!

Higgins, James, *Innovate or Evaporate*, New Management Publishing, 1995 – Kind of academic about the topic but worth reading.

Higgins, James, *101 Creative Problem Solving Techniques*, New Management Publishing, 1994 – Another re-hash of the old techniques.

Hirshberg, Jerry, *The Creative Priority*, Harper Business, 1998 – The story about Nissan Design International which is a must read for those interested in creating an environment for creativity and innovation in their organizations.

Kao, John, *Jamming*, Harper Business, 1996 – Not very exciting at all but he's a jazz musician and can't be all that bad.

Kawasaki, Guy, *Rules for Revolutionaries*, Harper Business, 1998 – Fun to read and a lot of different thinking.

Kriegel, Robert, *If It Ain't Broke - Break It*, Warner, 1991 – Some good contrarian thinking and it's lots of fun.

Land, George, *Breakpoint and Beyond*, Harper Business, 1992 – There's some great stuff in here and I highly recommend it.

MacKenzie, Gordon, *Orbiting the Giant Hairball*, Viking, 1996 – Very entertaining stories about his years with Hallmark.

Mattimore, Bryan, *99% Inspiration*, Amacom, 1993 – Pretty good read.

McGartland, Grace, *Thunderbolt Thinking*, Bernard-Davis, 1994 – Cute title, cute book, but there was no lightning at all.

Metcalf, C.W., *Lighten Up*, Addison Wesley, 1992 – One of my favorite people at his best.

Michalko, Michael, *Thinkertoys*, Ten Speed Press, 1991 – This is a best selling book and is a good source of techniques for thinking creatively.

Michalko, Michael, *Cracking Creativity*, Ten Speed Press, 1988 – Well written with good references to creative thinkers from the past.

Meyer, Pamela, *Quantum Creativity*, Yezand Press, 1997 – A different look at creativity from someone with an improvisational theatre background.

Miller, William, *The Creative Edge*, Addison Wesley, 1986 – Much to perfect for me.

Mingo, Jack, *How the Cadillac Got Its Fins*, Harper Collins, 1994 – Another fun read about tales from the annals of business.

Morrison, Ian, *The Second Curve*, Ballantine Books, 1996 – This is in a class with The Fifth Discipline. One of the best books on change I've ever read.

Nadler, Gerald, *Breakthrough Thinking*, Prima Publishing, 1990 – There was no breakthrough here for me. Save your money.

Nayak and Ketteringham, *Breakthroughs*, Rawson Associates, 1986 – Good source of stories about innovation.

Popcorn, Faith, *The Popcorn Report*, Doubleday Currency, 1992 – An interesting look at trends.

Popcorn, Faith, *Clicking*, Harper Collins, 1996, Ditto.

Prahalad and Hamel, *Competing for the Future*, Harvard Business School Press1994 – A great book! Read it two or three times!

Ray, Michael, *Creativity in Business*, Doubleday, 1986 – Well worth reading even though it's a bit on the old side.

Ray, Michael, *The Creative Spirit*, Dutton, 1992 – Save your money.

Ray, Michael, *The Path of the Everyday Hero*, Jeremy Tarcher, 1991 – I never got to use my highlight once.

Ricchiuto, Jack, *Collaborative Creativity*, Oakhill Press, 1997, - Has a few good points in it.

Robinson, Alan, *Corporate Creativity*, Berrett-Koehler, 1997 – Written by a couple of professors and shows it. There is nothing workable here at all.

Rich, Ben E., *Skunk Works*, Little, Brown, and Co, 1994 – Hard to put down. Contains some terrific stories of the Lockheed skunkworks that somehow produced some wonderful aircraft.

Roberts, Royston, Serendipity, John Wiley & Sons, 1989 – Some good stories about discovery.

Robert & Weiss, *The Innovation Formula*, Ballinger Publishing, 1988 – A little text booky but worth taking a look at.

Schwartz, Peter, *The Art of the Long View*, Double Currency, 1991 – One of the best books around on the topic of scenarios.

Senge, Peter, *The Fifth Discipline*, Doubleday Currency, 1990 – A definite classic to be read twice.

Sieden, Lloyd, *Buckminster Fuller's Universe*, Plenum Press, 1989 – Good book about a great mind!

Tanner, David, *Total Creativity in Business and Industry*, 1997 – A good book for putting you to sleep. Save your money.

Thompson, Chic, *What a Great Idea!*, Harper Perennial, 1992 – Some pretty good stuff here.

Thompson, Chic, *Yes, But*, Harper Business, 1992 – A fun book with a few tidbits in it.

Tucker, Robert, *Managing the Future*, Putnam & Sons, 1991 – A good read especially for those who want to manage the future by pushing today forward.

Van Gundy, *Idea Power*, Amacom, 1992 – Andy was a good friend (he recently passed on) and he is probably the ultimate technique guy.

Van Gundy, *Brain Boosters for Business Advantage*, Pfeiffer & Co., 1995 – A definite buy!

von Oech, Roger, *A Whack on the Side of the Head*, Harper & Row, 1983 – Both of von Oech's book are classics even though they are quite dated.

von Oech, Roger, *A Kick in the Seat of the Pants*, Harper & Row, 1986

Weller, Tom, *The Book of Stupid Questions*, Warner Books, 1988 – There are some books you should have for absolutely no reason at all. This is one of them.

Wujec, Tom, *Five Star Mind*, Doubleday, 1995 – There's a lot of good stuff here and it's fun to read.

Wycoff, Joyce, *Transformation Thinking*, Berkley Books, 1995 – There's a few tidbits here.

Wycoff, Joyce, *Mindmapping,* Berkley Books, 1991 – Good book on the topic.

# Appendix G

# New job titles

In my workshops I often ask people to give themselves new job titles that inspire them to be different. Here are examples of some of these titles (and a few that have appeared in Fast Company magazine). Feel free to use them as your own title. Would you rather be a manger, a director, or a *Wicked Good Slayer of Organizational Sacred Cows?*

- Chief Gadfly

- Sorcerer's Apprentice

- Purveyor of Outrageously Interesting Ideas

- Rattler of Organizational Bushes

- Ruffler of Organizational Feathers

- Keeper of Pit Bulls for Mouth Foaming Creativity

- Zen Cat

- Purveyor of Feet in the Backside

- Slayer of Sacred Cows

- Mistress of Chaos

- Royal Keeper of Organizational Stardust

- Yah-Butt Blaster

- Supreme Allied Commander
- Mind Mine Sweeper
- Supreme Strategic Processtologist
- Catcher of All That Hits Fans
- Wild Thing
- Sand Box Monitor
- Management Heel Nipper
- Happily Ever After Maker
- Empress of the Universe
- Resident Disturber of the Peace
- Raging Inexorable Thunder-Lizard Evangelist
- Organizational Terrorist & Demolitionist
- Wild thing
- Supreme Allied Commander
- Wicked Good Consultant
- All That Is Powerful and Wise
- Big Kahuna
- Muckety Muck
- Duchess of Danger
- Paid Renegade

- Troublemaker
- Director of Fun
- Resultant
- Troublemaker
- Master of Madness
- Vibe Evolver
- Pride Piper of Creativity
- Wicker Good Idea Generator
- Idea Steward
- Idea Gooser
- Chief Creatologist
- Myth Debunker
- Resident Dreamer
- Seer, Inspirer, and Spark Plug
- Wizard of Wonder
- Resident Disturber of the Peace
- Hope Builder
- Liberator of Fools
- Super Simplifier
- Hierarchy Saboteur

- Cerebral proctologist
- Innovation Evangelist
- Chief Imagination Officer
- Insight Manager
- Human Being
- Chief Imagination Officer
- Control Czar
- Director of Everything
- Chief Humor Officer
- Squeezer of Organizational Thinking Juices
- Manager of Mischief
- Resultant

# Appendix H

## Things to *Whine* About

Are you thinking of having a **W*hine and Jeez Party***? Okay, here's a chance to get it out of your system once and for all. Repeat after me:

1.  We tried that before.
2.  We're different.
3.  It cost too much.
4.  That's not my job.
5.  They're too busy to do that.
6.  We don't have the time.
7.  We don't have enough help.
8.  It's too radical a change.
9.  The staff will never buy it.
10. It's against company policy.
11. The union will scream.
12. It'll run up our overhead.
13. We don't have the authority.
14. Let's get back to reality.
15. That's not our problem.
16. I don't like the idea.
17. You're right, but ….
18. You're two years behind the times.
19. We're not ready for that.
20. It isn't in the budget.
21. You can't teach an old dog new tricks.
22. Good thought, but impractical.
23. Let's give it more thought.

24. We'll be the laughing stock of the industry.
25. Not that again.
26. Where did you dig that one up?
27. We did all right without it.
28. It's never been tried before.
29. Let's put that on the back burner for now.
30. Let's form a committee
31. I don't see the connection.
32. It won't work in our office.
33. The executive committee would never go for it.
34. Let's all sleep on it.
35. It can't be done.
36. It's too much trouble to change.
37. It won't pay for itself.
38. It's impossible.
39. I know a person who tried it and …
40. We've always done it this way.
41. Top management won't buy it.
42. We'd lose money in the long run.
43. Don't rock the boat.
44. That's what we can expect from staff.
45. Has anyone else ever tried it?
46. Let's look into it further (later).
47. Quit dreaming.
48. Our plate's too full now.
49. It's too much work.
50. Let's have another meeting on it.

# Appendix I

# Murphy's Laws of Combat Operations

Finally, let me leave you with something I've had in my files for years. I have no idea where it came from but I'm sure it will trigger some interesting thoughts for you. It has for me. Isn't it interesting how close organizational dynamics is to combat operations?

1.  Military intelligence can be a contradiction in terms
2.  Recoilless rifles – aren't.
3.  A sucking chest wound is nature's way of telling you to slow down own.
4.  The enemy diversion you are ignoring is the main attack.
5.  If the enemy is within range, so are you.
6.  Friendly fire – isn't.
7.  If it is a stupid idea and it works, then it isn't stupid.
8.  When you have a secure area don't forget to tell the enemy.
9.  If you are short of everything, except the enemy, then you're in the combat zone.
10. Try to look unimportant. They may be low on ammo.
11. The easy way is always mined
12. Tracers work both ways.
13. Incoming fire has the right of way.
14. Teamwork is essential. It gives them other people to shoot at.
15. Never draw fire. It irritates everyone around you.
16. No combat ready unit has ever passed inspection.
17. No inspection ready unit has ever passed combat.
18. Make it too tough for the enemy to get in and you can't get out.

19. If both sides are convinced they're about to lose, they're both right.
20. Professionals are predictable, but the world is full of dangerous amateurs.
21. Fortify your front and you'll get your rear shot up.
22. When in doubt, empty your magazine.
23. In war, important things are simple, and all simple things are hard.
24. Don't look conspicuous – it draws fire.
25. Communications will fail as soon as you need fire support desperately.
26. Weather ain't neutral.
27. Never share a foxhole with anyone braver than you.
28. Remember, your weapon was made by the lowest bidder.
29. If you can't remember, the Claymore is pointed towards you.
30. All five-second grenade fuses are three seconds.
31. The only thing more accurate than incoming enemy fire is incoming friendly fire.
32. If your attack is going really well, it's an ambush.
33. No operation plan survives first contact intact.
34. If it flies, it dies.
35. When you are forward of your position, the artillery will always be short.
36. Suppressive fire – won't.
37. You are not superman.
38. Calvary doesn't always come to the rescue.
39. B-52's are the ultimate in close air support.
40. Sniper's motto is, reach out and touch someone.
41. Peace is our profession – mass murder is just a hobby.
42. Killing for peace is like whoring for virginity.
43. It's not the one with your name on it – it's the round addressed "to whom it may concern" you've got to worry about.
44. Remember – Napalm is an area weapon.

45. Smart bombs have bad days too.
46. Mines are equal opportunity weapons.
47. There is no such thing as a perfect plan.

# Appendix J

# Interesting Facts

Following are some facts that may surprise you. Pick some and play with them a bit. What possibilities do they bring to mind regarding an opportunity of your own?

1.  You're in Paris and you decide to use your AMEX. Getting credit approval involves a 46,000 mile journey over phones and computers. The job is done in 5 seconds! - Peter Large, Micro Revolution Revisited

2.  The EINIAC, commonly thought of as the first modern computer, was built in 1944. It took up more space than an 18-wheeler's tractor-trailer, weighed more than 17 Chevrolet Camaros, and consumed 140,000 watts of electricity. Einiac could execute up to 5,000 basic arithmetic operations per second.

3.  One of today's popular microprocessors, the 486, is built on a tiny piece of silicon about the size of a dime. It weighs less than a packet of sweet and low, and uses less than 2 watts of electricity. A 486 can execute up to 54,000,000 instructions per second!

4.  Computer power is now 8,000 times less expensive than it was 30 years ago. If we had similar progress in automotive technology, today you could buy a Lexus for about $2. It would travel at the speed of sound, and go about 600 miles on a thimble of gas. - John Naisbitt, Global Paradox

5.  At the rate of one execution per day, it would take seven years to execute everyone who is on death row in the United States.

6.  The US has 70% of the world's lawyers, one per 335 people. In Japan the ratio is one per every 9000 people.

7.  The nucleus accounts for almost all the atom's solidarity yet occupies one million millionth of its total volume. The rest is empty space (with electrons spinning around). Bodies are mostly empty space. The solid matter for all the human bodies on earth lumped together would be no bigger than a pea. The solid matter for the entire world would fit inside a football stadium!

8.  The entire continent of Africa has fewer phones than the city of Tokyo.

9.  Farmington, Maine is the Earmuff Capital of the World. Chester Greenwood invented them in 1873 at age 13.

10. The distance between the wing tips of a Boeing 747 is longer than the Wright Brothers' first flight.

11. In 1977, US carmakers actually recalled more vehicles than they produced.

12. If every fax owner switched to ½ page cover sheets instead of a full page, it would save nearly 2 million miles of un-recyclable fax paper annually.

13. Some natural shampoos and toothpastes are no different than industrial strength cleaners - they rely on detergents to break

down grease. Unfortunately, detergents break down human cell walls as well and are thought by some to be carcinogenic.

14. Cushioned heels may be good for your body and soles, but shoes with leather uppers are laced with residual chromium. Worse, highly toxic lead accounts for 2 to 3% of the polyvinyl chloride used in the soles of some shoes.

15. Gas-guzzlers are harder on the environment than electric cars, right? Wrong! A conventional car creates 26 tons of hazardous waste for every ton the vehicle weighs. A battery-powered automobile produces twice as much 0 52 tons, including a witches' brew of lead and toxic acids.

16. Boob tubes contain more than 4,000 chemicals, some of which you inhale while watching (because of off-gassing). In addition, since each set contains 18-20 grams of toxic mercury, driving a truckload of TV's would qualify you as a toxic waste hauler.

17. Your favorite jeans may be 100% cotton, but that doesn't make them 100% pure. While cotton amounts to only 3% of the world's crops, its cultivation consumes 26% of the world's tonnage of pesticides.

18. No matter what their contents, aluminum cans can't be completely recycled into new aluminum cans - the recycled aluminum is too impure. So every year millions of pounds of hazardous slag are shipped to waste dumps in third world countries.

19. The combined wealth of the world's 358 billionaires now equals the total income of the poorest 45 percent of the

world's population, some 2.3 billion people. (United *Nations' Human Development Report 1996*)

20. On a Canadian two-dollar bill the flag flying over the Parliament Building is an American flag.

21. Both diamond and graphite are composed of only carbon atoms, but because of different pattern, diamond is the hardest substance known and graphite is one of the softest.

22. The patent for the fax machine was issued 30 years before the telephone in 1843 and the first commercial fax was sent in 1865.

23. A nanometer is to a pebble as a pebble is to the earth's diameter.

24. Using 50 nanometer pits on a CD rather than the current size (10 square micrometers) would allow you to get the equivalent of 1000 CD's on the size of a wristwatch.

25. Let's say you're going to a party, so you pull out some pocket change and buy a little greeting card that plays "Happy Birthday" when it's opened. After the party, someone casually tosses the card into the trash, throwing away more computer power than existed in the entire world before 950.

26. No word in the English language rhymes with month, silver, orange, or purple.

27. The home video camera you use to take pictures contains more processing power than an old IBM 360, the wonder machine that gave birth to the mainframe computer age. And the Saturn system made by game maker, Sega, runs on a

higher-performance processor than the original 1976 Cray supercomputer that in its day was accessible only to the most elite physicists.

28. The average vocabulary has 8000 words. The average supermarket has over 12,000 brands.

29. Peanuts are one of the ingredients of dynamite.

30. Rubber bands last longer when refrigerated.

31. Charley Chaplin once entered a Charlie Chaplin look-alike contest and came in third!

32. Spiders' silk has long been used in the lenses of gun sites and surveying instruments. It is finer and stronger than anything made by man. One pound of spider web would stretch fifteen thousand miles.

33. Almonds are members of the peach family.

34. A dragonfly has a life span of 24 hours and a goldfish has a memory span of 3 seconds.

35. In England, the Speaker of the House is not allowed to speak.

36. A single pair of fruit flies in just one year can produce 700 to 800 offspring. Wow, that a lot of diapers!

37. An estimated 5 million trillion bacteria live on Earth and they have a combined weight roughly equal to the top 3 feet of France.

38. Ever wonder how big a trillion is? If you had a stack of one-thousand-dollar bills totaling $1 million in front of you it would be about 3 inches high. A billion dollars in one-thousand-dollar bills would reach about 250 feet. One trillion dollars would be a little over forty-seven miles high!

39. Two human eyes have more information processing capacity than all the supercomputers in the world

# About the Author

Lindsay Collier presently resides in The Villages, Florida with his wife, Jean. After serving as a Captain in the US Army Corps of Engineers he joined Eastman Kodak as an engineer and took an early retirement after 25 years. During his tenure at Kodak he became their expert in creative thinking and innovation and went on to become an author, speaker and consultant after his retirement. He has shared his ideas with many organizations in the United States and abroad in the form of books, workshops, and keynote presentations.

Lindsay is available on a limited basis for speaking engagements on the topic of this book as well as a number of other topics. His talks are chock full of great information along with some great humor. He can be contacted at lindsaycollier@comcast.net.

His webpage (which he calls his *thinkorarium*) is at
**lindsaycollier.weebly.com**
and his Amazon author page is
**amazon.com/author/lindsaycollier.**

## Other books by Lindsay Collier

The Whack-A-Mole Theory; Creating Breakthrough and
Transformation in Organizations

Get Out of Your Thinking Box; 365 Ways to Brighten Your Life
and Enhance Your Creativity

Jan's Rainbow; Stories of Hope; How Those You Have Lost Stay
in Touch With You.

### EBooks:

Surviving Loss of A Loved One: Jan's Rainbow
Quotations to Tickle Your Brain
How to Live Happily Ever After (Kindle Short)
Organizational Braindroppings; Musings on Organizational
Breakthrough and Change